MW0416068

KNOW THYSELF

100 Guided Meditations on Humility of Heart

PRESENTED TO

NAME

DATE / OCCASION

PERSONAL NOTE

KNOW THYSELF

100 Guided Meditations on Humility of Heart

Adapted from the writings of Rev. Fr. Cajetan da Bergamo
With thoughts from the saints, prayers and scripture readings

Edited and compiled by
Ryan Grant

TAN Books
Charlotte, North Carolina

Know Thyself: 100 Guided Meditations on Humility of Heart
© 2018 TAN Books

This compilation is derived from the TAN Edition of *Humility of Heart* by Fr. Cajetan Mary da Bergamo, Capuchin, 1660-1753, Translated from the Italian by Herbert Cardinal Vaughan, 1832-1903. First published circa 1905. Published by TAN Books in 1978 by photographic reproduction from a 1944 reprint edition of Newman Bookshop, Westminster, Maryland. Selected, retypeset, with minor copy editing, and republished by TAN Books in 2006. Quotes from saints and prayers compiled from public domain sources.

Cover & interior design by David Ferris, www.davidferrisdesign.com

Sacred Heart cover image adapted from Holy card, dedicated to the Sacred Heart, 1906 (printed card), French School, (19th century)/ Private Collection/Bridgeman Images

ISBN: 978-1-50511-286-3

Published in the United States by

TAN Books
PO Box 410487
Charlotte, NC 28241

www.TANBooks.com

Printed in the United States of America

Virtus humilitatis augeatur obtrunceturque vitium superbiæ omnibus membris Ecclessiæ militantis.

†

In all the members of the Church militant, may the virtue of humility might be increased and the vice of pride and all evils flowing from it might be extinguished.

TABLE OF CONTENTS

INTRODUCTION

The spiritual writers assure us that humility is the foundation virtue, the beginning of the spiritual life, the thing necessary for our prayers to have any merit whatsoever, and so on. There are many sentiments of the saints in regard to our need for humility. St. Augustine of Hippo tells us: "In the soul where this virtue does not exist, there cannot be any other virtue except in mere appearance." St. Thomas Aquinas notes that "humility properly regards the subjection of man to God."[1] St. Cyprian says it is "the foundation of sanctity." St. Jerome says it is "the first Christian virtue." St. Elizabeth Anne Seton warns us that: "The gate of Heaven is very low; only the humble can enter it." Conversely, pride, the vice opposite to humility, is the font of all vices, just as humility is the foundation of all virtues.

Yet, what really is humility? We can quote scholastic definitions, or the catechism, and these are all important and have their place. Nevertheless, do these tell us what humility is for every man, a clear do this and you will attain it? Interestingly, no, because the self-same virtue must also be applied to each and every individual, and he may do acts that for him are true acts of humility, and for another man would be the height of pride. Humility is a virtue which carries with it a lot of apparent contradictions. On the one hand I must possess it, on the other hand, if I think I have it then I am not truly humble. Then, there are those who inadvertently cultivate a false humility, because they take pride in trying to practice humility

---

1 St. Thomas Aquinas, *Summa Theologica,* II-II, q. 162, a. 1c

in their actions, and feel even more pride when some-one notices. Others imagine they are humble because they have many virtues, and it seems to them as they must possess humility then, when really they don't. It is said that in the ancient world the philosopher Plato invited the philosopher Diogenes to dinner. Diogenes made it a doctrine to despise gold, the trappings of wealth and power, as well as worldly gain. When he appeared in Plato's house in his filthy rags, he noticed expensive drapery had been hung up. Then, the humble dinner guest tore one down and stamped on it. "What are you doing?" Plato inquired. "I am trampling Plato's pride," was the reply. To this, Plato answered: "You are indeed, but in doing so you are showing your own pride, but in another way."

This paradox of humility often confronts those embarking on the spiritual life. If knowing I am humble means I am not actually humble at all, and knowing I am prideful usually means I am actually quite proud, how in the world does any man attain humility?

The process is a daily battle, and does not have an end. It is said of St. John Vianney that the devil came to tempt him to pride on his death bed, but while the devil was in the process of praising the saint for how humble he was, his retort was, "I'm not dead yet." Certainly the holy Curé had developed the virtue of humility, but he was blessedly unaware of it, and even at the moment of death was still working on cultivating this virtue.

This book, *Know Thyself* is intended to assist the reader in the same process. The meditations are drawn from

Cardinal Bergamo's *Humility of Heart*, lightly edited and arranged in logical order as well as combined with a quote from a saint. An appendix has also been provided with scripture quotes as well as prayers from the Church and saints to assist you in examining every aspect of your life where you could go astray on the path to humility. Frequent meditation in this area will help us whittle away our own contradictions, see our hidden vanities, and root out our false expressions of humility and virtue. The thoughts and meditations contained here will help a man in any state of life examine himself frequently so that, reminded again and again, he may make his life an imitation of the virtue of humility in Christ. Indeed, if Christ is God, yet chose to empty himself and take the form of man, what right have we, dust and ashes, to think so highly of ourselves? Every last thing in this work points to Christ, meek and humble of heart, Who would have us share in His humility if we are willing to enter into the combat.

—The Editor

MEDITATIONS

MEDITATION 1

If men would consider how glorious a thing it is to
imitate in this life the humility of the Son of God, and
would picture to themselves to what a height of glory this
humility would lead them, we should find very few proud
men. But since the majority of men measure everything
by their senses and by human considerations, we must not
be astonished if the number of the humble is small,
and the number of the proud infinite.

—St. Robert Bellarmine

❧ † ☙

Jesus Christ calls us all into His school to learn, not to work miracles nor to astonish the world by marvelous enterprises, but to be humble of heart. "Learn of Me, because I am meek and humble of heart" *(Matthew 11:29)*. He has not called every one to be doctors, preachers or priests, nor has He bestowed on all the gift of restoring sight to the blind, healing the sick, raising the dead or casting out devils, but to all He has said: "Learn of Me to be humble of heart," and to all He has given the power to learn humility of Him. Innumerable things are worthy of imitation in the Incarnate Son of God, but He only asks us to imitate His humility. What then? Must we suppose that all the treasures of Divine Wisdom which were in Christ are to be reduced to the virtue of humility? Humility contains all things because in this virtue is truth; therefore God must also dwell therein, since He is the truth.

The Savior might have said: "Learn of Me to be chaste, humble, prudent, just, wise, abstemious, etc." But He only says: "Learn of Me, because I am meek and humble of heart;" and in humility alone He includes all things, because as St. Thomas so truly says, "Acquired humility is in a certain sense the greatest good." Therefore, whoever possesses this virtue may be said, as to his proximate disposition, to possess all virtues, and he who lacks it, lacks all.

MEDITATION 2

We must never glance at what is good in ourselves,
much less ponder over it, but we should search out
what is wrong and what is lacking. This is an
excellent way of remaining humble.

—St. Vincent de Paul

≈ † ≈

There is a kind of humility which is of counsel and of perfection such as that which desires and seeks the contempt of others; but there is also a humility which is of necessity and of precept, without which, says Christ, we cannot enter into the kingdom of heaven: "Thou shalt not enter into the kingdom of heaven" *(Matthew 18:3)*. And this consists in not esteeming ourselves and in not wishing to be esteemed by others above what we really are.

No one can deny this truth, that humility is essential to all those who wish to be saved. "No one reaches the kingdom of heaven except by humility," says St. Augustine.

But I ask, what is practically this humility which is so necessary? When we are told that faith and hope are necessary, it is also explained to us what we are to believe and to hope. In like manner, when humility is said to be necessary, in what should its practice consist except in the lowest opinion of ourselves? It is in this moral sense that the humility of the heart has been explained by the fathers of the Church. But can I say with truth that I possess this humility which I recognize as necessary and obligatory? What care or solicitude do I display to acquire it?

How and when do I practice its acts, acknowledging and confessing my unworthiness before God? The following was the frequent prayer of St. Augustine, "Noscam Te, noscam me—May I know Thee; may I know myself!" and by this prayer he asked for humility, which is nothing else but a true knowledge of God and of oneself. To confess that God is what He is, the Omnipotent God, "Great is the Lord, and exceedingly to be praised," *(Psalm 47:1 [48])* and to declare that we are but nothingness before Him: "My substance is as nothing before Thee" *(Psalm 38 [39]:6)*, this is to be humble.

MEDITATION 3

Certainly nothing can so effectually humble us before the mercy of God as the multitude of His benefits. Nor can anything so much humble us before His justice as the enormity of our innumerable offences. Let us consider what He has done for us and what we have done against Him.

—St. Francis de Sales

❧ † ☙

What should we say if we saw the public executioner walking in the streets and claiming to be esteemed, respected and honored? We should consider his effrontery as insufferable as his calling is infamous. And you, my soul, each time that you have sinned mortally you have indeed been as an executioner, nailing to the cross the Son of God! Thus St. Paul describes sinners "crucifying again to themselves the Son of God" *(Hebrews 6:6)*.

And with this character of infamy which you bear within yourself, do you still dare to demand honor and esteem? Will you still have the courage to say: "I insist upon being honored and respected, I will not be slighted?" However much pride may tempt me to boast and seek esteem, I have ample cause to blush with shame when I hear the voice of conscience reproaching me for my ignominy and my sins, and not ceasing to reprove me for being a perfidious and ungrateful rebel against God, a traitor and

11

an executioner who co-operated in the passion and death of Jesus Christ. "All the day long my shame is before me, and the confusion of my face hath covered me at the voice of him that reproacheth me" *(Psalm 43 [44]: 16-17).*

MEDITATION 4

*Since it has been given to me too, to understand the love
of the Heart of Jesus, I own that it has chased all fear from
mine! The remembrance of my faults humiliates me, and
urges me never to depend upon my own strength which is
nothing but weakness: still more does this remembrance
speak to me of mercy and of love. When, with all filial
confidence we cast our faults into the devouring furnace
of love, how should they not be totally consumed?*

—St. Therese of Lisieux

✤ † ✤

We must acknowledge that one of the five reasons
why we do not live in this necessary humility is
because we do not fear the justice of God. Look at a criminal, how humbly he stands before the judge, with low-
ered eyes, pallid face and bowed head: he knows that he
has been convicted of atrocious crimes; he knows that
thereby he has merited capital punishment, and may justly
be condemned to the gallows, and hence he fears, and his
fear keeps him humble, chasing from his brain all thought
of ambition and vain-glory. So the soul, conscious of the
numerous sins it has committed, aware that it has indeed
deserved hell, and that from one moment to another it
may be condemned to hell by divine justice, fears the

wrath of God, and this fear causes the soul to remain humble before Him; and if it does not feel this humility, it can only be because the fear of God is wanting: "There is no fear of God before his eyes" *(Psalm 35 [36]:1)*. Oh, cry to God from your heart: "Pierce Thou my flesh with Thy fear" *(Psalm 118 [119]:120)*.

And this holy fear which is the beginning of wisdom will also be the beginning of true humility; for as the inspired Word says, humility and wisdom are inseparable companions: "Where humility is, there also is wisdom" *(Proverbs 11:2)*.

MEDITATION 5

Be careful to give no credit to yourself for anything;
if you do, you are stealing from God, to whom
alone every good thing is due.

—St. Vincent de Paul

❧ ✝ ❧

There is no saint however holy and innocent who may not truly consider himself the greatest sinner in the world. It is enough that he knows himself to be man to recognize that he is liable to commit all the evil of which man is capable. As man, I have in my corrupt nature a proclivity to every evil; and so far as I am concerned I am quite capable of committing all kinds of sin, and if I do not commit them it is through a special grace of God which preserves and restrains me.

A tree does not fall while bending under its own weight, and this must be attributed to the strength of its support; and in the same way if I have not fallen into every kind of iniquity, it must not be attributed to my own inherent virtue but only to divine grace, which by its goodness has supported me. Therefore, how can I regard myself more than another man while we are all equal in human weakness? "For what is my strength?" *(Job 6:11)*. I am a son of Adam like every other man, born in sin, inclined to sin, and ever ready to fall into sin. I have no need of the devil to tempt me to sin; my own concupis-cence is only too great a temptation; and if God were to withdraw from me His protecting and helping hand, I know that I should be precipitated headlong from bad to worse.

When St. Augustine made his examination of con-science, he did not always find it sufficient to excite within him sorrow and contrition, so he dwelt on those sins which he might or would have committed had he not been preserved from them by God's infinite mercy; and he grieved and accused himself and humbly implored pardon of God for the evil capacity he had to commit all kinds of heinous and impious sins. In this practice is to be found an exercise of true humility.

MEDITATION 6

Let it be assured that to do no wrong is really
super-human, and belongs to God alone.

—*St. Gregory Nazianzen.*

✣

It has often happened that those who were more perfect than others have shamefully fallen, and this after a long period of good and virtuous works, showing the marvelous things that a man can do when helped by God's special grace, and who by their terrible fall have also testified to the iniquities of which a man is capable if abandoned to himself and left to the weakness of his own free-will.

God has shown His creative omnipotence by forming me out of nothing and making me a human being. Were God to withdraw his omnipotent preserving hand from me I should at once show that I am capable of when left to myself, by returning immediately into my nothingness. And, in the order of grace, the nothingness into which I relapse when left to myself is sin. How often "I am brought to nothing, and I knew not" *(Psalm 72 [73]: 21)*. And what can I find to be proud of in that nothingness?

Give me grace, O my God, to know myself only as much as is necessary to keep me humble! for if I fully realized the insignificance of my own being and the extent of my malice which is capable of offending You in diverse inconceivable ways, I fear that I should be so filled with horror at myself that I should give in to despair!

We have within ourselves, in our own experience and feelings, a knowledge of how greatly our frail and fallen nature is inclined to evil. Today we go and confess certain of our faults, making the resolution not to fall into them again, and tomorrow notwithstanding we commit them once more.

At one moment we make up our minds to acquire a certain virtue and the next we do just the contrary by falling into the opposite vice. Then we make these resolutions of amendment and we imagine that our will is firm and strong, but we soon perceive how weak and unreliable it is, for we behave as though we had never purposed amendment at all.

Our heart is like a reed that bends before every wind, or a boat tossed by every wave. It is enough to meet with an occasion of sin, a movement of passion, a breath of temptation, for the will to yield to evil even when in certain moments of fervor, we seem most firmly rooted in good.

When this occurs, it would be well to say: O my God, I can do all things if I am strengthened by Your help; but without it I can do nothing, nor will I ever be able to do anything! Not only without You can I never do any meritorious act of virtue whatsoever, but I cannot do anything at all; as St. Augustine instructs me: "Whether it be little or whether it be great, it cannot be done without Him."

MEDITATION 7

*Pride is an illusion, a lie and a theft. And since
it is a truth of faith that we are nothing, he who
esteems himself and thinks that he is someone
is a seducer who deceives himself.*

–St. John Eudes

❦ † ❦

We may persuade ourselves that we possess various
virtues because we have a tangible proof within us
that we really have them. Thus we may judge ourselves
to be chaste, because we feel really attracted to chastity;
or we may think ourselves abstemious, because we are so
by nature; or obedient, because we practice a ready obedience. But however much a man may exercise humility,
he can never form any judgement as to his being really
humble, for he who thinks himself humble is no longer so.

In the same way that to recognize that we are proud
is the beginning of humility, so to flatter ourselves that
we are humble is the beginning of pride, and the more
humble we think ourselves the greater is our pride. That
self-complacency which the heart feels, making us imagine that we are humble in consequence of some agree-
able reflections we have had about ourselves, is a species
of vanity; and how can vanity exist with humility which

is founded solely on truth? Vanity is nothing but a lie, and it is precisely from a lie that pride springs.

Let us pray to God with the prophet: "Let not the foot of pride come to me" *(Psalm 35 [36]:12)*. Grant O my God, that I may be humble. Make me holy, yet ignorant of holiness; for if I should learn how to know or even to imagine myself holy, I should become vain; and through vanity should lose all humility and holiness.

MEDITATION 8

Let humility be always at work, like the bee at the honeycomb, or all will be lost. But remember, the bee leaves its hive to fly in search of flowers and the soul should sometimes cease thinking of itself to rise in meditation on the grandeur and majesty of its God. It will learn its own baseness better thus than by self-contemplation, and will be freer from the reptiles which enter the first room where self-knowledge is acquired. Although it is a great grace from God to practice self-examination, "yet too much is as bad as too little," as they say; believe me, by God's help, we shall advance more by contemplating the Divinity than by keeping our eyes fixed on ourselves, poor creatures of earth that we are.

—St. Teresa of Ávila

✤ † ✤

It is possible that a tormenting doubt might arise in the mind of some one who might say: If I must judge myself to be wanting in humility, I must conclude that I am lost, and such a judgement would lead me to despair. But do you not perceive the error?

To speak wisely you ought to say: I know I am wanting in humility; therefore I must try and obtain it; for without humility I am a reprobate, and it is necessary to be humble in order to be among the elect.

There would indeed be cause for despair if on the one hand humility were necessary for salvation and on the other it were unattainable. But nothing is more natural to us than humility, because we are drawn towards it by our own misery; and nothing is easier, since it is enough for us to open our eyes and to know ourselves; this is not a virtue we need go far to seek, as we can always find it within ourselves, and we have an infinity of good reasons in ourselves for doing so. Nevertheless, we must labor as long as life lasts to acquire humility, nor must we ever imagine that we have acquired it; arid even should we have obtained it in some degree, we must still continue to strive after it as though we did not possess it, in order that we maybe able to keep it. Let us have a true desire to be humble; let us not cease to implore God that He may give us the grace to be humble; and let us often study the motives that may help to make us humble of heart; and let us not doubt the divine Goodness, but conform to the advice given us in Holy Writ: "Think of the Lord in goodness" *(Wisdom 1:1)*.

MEDITATION 9

*I cannot say that Our Lord makes me walk in the way
of exterior humiliation; He is satisfied with humbling
me in my inmost soul. In the eyes of creatures all
is success, and I walk in the dangerous path of
honor—if a religious may so speak.*

—St. Thérèse of Lisieux

☙ † ☙

Although we feel the humiliation keenly when we
are insulted, persecuted or calumniated, this does not
mean that we cannot suffer such trials with sentiments of
true humility, subjecting nature to reason and faith and sac-
rificing the resentment of our self-love to the love of God.

We are not made of stone, so that we need be insen-
sible or senseless in order to be humble. Of some martyrs
we read that they writhed under their torments; of others
that they more or less rejoiced in them, according to the
greater or less degree of unction they received from the
Holy Spirit; and all were rewarded by the crown of glory,
as it is not the pain or the feeling that makes the martyr but
the supernatural motive of virtue. In the same way some
humble persons feel pleasure in being humiliated, and
some feel sadness, especially when weighed down with
calumny; and yet they all belong to the sphere of the humble, because it is not the humiliation, nor the suffering

alone which makes the soul humble, but the interior act by which this same humiliation is accepted and received through motives of Christian humility and especially of a desire to resemble Jesus Christ, who, though entitled to all the honors the world could offer Him, bore humiliation and scorn for the glory of His eternal Father: "For Thy sake, O God of Israel, I have borne reproach" *(Psalm 68 [69]: 9).*

The doctrine of St. Bernard is worthy of our notice: It is one thing to be humiliated, and another to be humble. It often happens that the proud man is humiliated, yet he nevertheless remains proud, receiving humiliations with anger and contempt, doing all he can to escape them with fretful impatience. It sometimes happens too that the proud man becomes humble; the humiliation teaching him to know himself as he is, and by this knowledge he learns to love this very humiliation: "He is humble who converts all his humiliations into humility and says unto God: 'It is good for me that Thou hast humbled me'" *(Serm. 34 in Cant).*

MEDITATION 10

*His Majesty can do nothing greater for us than grant us
a life which is an imitation of that lived by His Beloved
Son. I feel certain, therefore, that these favors are given us to
strengthen our weakness, as I have sometimes said here, so
that we may be able to imitate Him in His great sufferings.*

−St. Teresa of Ávila

❧ † ❧

In a country where all are blind it is sufficient for a man
to have but one eye for him to be said to have good
sight, and amongst a multitude of ignorant people one
need possess but a slight tinge of knowledge to acquire
the reputation of being very learned; and in the same way
in this wicked and corrupt world it is easy to flatter ourselves that we are good, if we are not quite so bad as many
others. "I am not as the rest of men" *(Luke 18:11).* It was
in this way that the Pharisee praised himself in the temple.

But in order to know ourselves as we really are, it is
not with worldly-minded people that we ought to com-
pare ourselves, but with Jesus Christ, who is the model
for all those who are predestined. "Look," says St. Paul
to every one of us, quoting the words that were said to
Moses, "Look and make it according to the pattern that
was shown thee on the mount." How have I conformed
my life to the life of the Incarnate Son of God, who came

25

to teach me the way to heaven by His example? Ascend, O my soul, to the hill of Calvary, and gaze attentively upon thy crucified Savior! To this each one of us must conform in his own state of life if he wishes to be saved; such being the decree of the eternal Father, that the predestinated must be made conformable to the image of His Son. But can I truthfully and conscientiously say that I imitate Him? In what way? Let me examine myself. Ah, how different I am from Him! And what just cause I find in this examination to humble myself! In comparing myself with sinners I think myself a saint; but in comparing myself with Jesus Christ, whom I ought to imitate, I am compelled to acknowledge that I am a sinner and a reprobate; and the only consolation left to me is to trust in the infinite mercy of God. "O God, my support and my deliverer."

MEDITATION 11

Oh, how poor we seem when we examine our own
spirituality and goodness by the help of these reflections!
May it please God that we may not be like those men
who, dreaming that they possess great riches, awaken at the
point of death to find that they are only beggars: "They
have slept their sleep: and all the men of riches have found
nothing in their hands." May it please God that the plea
of our virtue may not prove an argument for our greater
condemnation: "And may that which is thought to be
progress in virtue not prove a cause of damnation."

—St. Gregory the Great

❧ † ☙

In order that an act of virtue be truly virtuous, it is necessary that it should be so in all its component parts, and
if it be defective on one point only it becomes vitiated at
once. A depraved intention, a single thought of vanity at
the beginning, middle or ending of any virtuous work is
sufficient to corrupt and change it into an evil one. It is
enough for virtue to be wanting in humility for this virtue,
which is no longer humble, to cease to be a virtue, and to
become a cause of moral pride.

It often happens to one who leads a spiritual life that
the more he strives after virtue, the more he finds a sweet

pleasure in himself, and therefore, as St. Augustine says, the sole fact of his self-satisfaction quickly renders him displeasing to God. "The more man thinks he has reason to be pleased with himself, so much the more I fear his self-esteem will displease God, who resists the proud" *(On Holy Virginity, ch. 34).*

MEDITATION 12

For mere ignorance, as in the first instance, does not
glory at all; and mere wisdom, as in the second, while
it has a kind of glory, yet does not glory in the Lord.
In the third evil case, however, man sins not in ignorance
but deliberately, usurping the glory which belongs to God.
And this arrogance is a more grievous and deadly fault
than the ignorance of the second, since it contemns God,
while the other knows Him not. Ignorance is brutal,
arrogance is devilish. Pride only, the chief of all iniquities,
can make us treat gifts as if they were rightful attributes
of our nature, and, while receiving benefits, rob our
Benefactor of His due glory.

–St. Bernard of Clairvaux

❦ † ❦

If we examine all of our falls into sin, whether venial or grave, the cause will always be found in some hidden pride; and true indeed are the words of the Holy Spirit: "For pride is the beginning of all sin" *(Matthew 7:7)*. Of this truth our Lord Jesus Christ Himself has warned us in His Gospel where he says: "And whosever shall exalt himself shall be humbled" *(Matthew 23:12)*. God and give no greater humiliation to a soul than to allow it to fall into sin; because sin is the lowest depth of all that is base, vile and shameful.

So each time that we are humbled by falling into sin, it is certain that we must previously have exalted ourselves by some act of pride; because only the proud are threatened with the punishment of this humiliation: "And he humbled himself afterwards, because his heart had been lifted up" *(Sirach 10:15)*. For thus it is written of King Hezekiah in holy Scripture, and the inspired writer has also said: "before destruction the heart of man is exalted" *(Proverbs 18:12)*.

Let us be so truly humble that we may not incur the punishment of this humiliation. No one can fall who lies on the ground; and no one can sin so long as he is humble. My God! My God! Let me remain in my nothingness, for it is the surest state for me.

MEDITATION 13

*Purity has its source in the heart, but it is in the body
that its material results take shape, and therefore it may be
forfeited both by the exterior senses and by the thoughts
and desires of the heart. All lack of modesty in seeing,
hearing, speaking, smelling, or touching, is impurity,
especially when the heart takes pleasure therein.*

—St. Francis de Sales

❧ † ☙

We read of many who, after being renowned for their
holiness, fervent in the exercise of prayer, great pen-
ances and signal virtues, and who, after being favored by
God with the gifts of ecstasy, revelations and miracles, have
nevertheless fallen into the hideous vice of impurity at the
slightest approach of temptation. And when I consider it, I
find that there is no sin that degrades the soul so much as
this impure sin of the senses, because the soul, from being
reasoning and spiritual, like the angels, becomes thereby
carnal, sensual and like brute beasts "who have no understanding" *(Psalm 31 [32]:9).*

I am constrained to adore with fear the supreme judgments of God and also for my own warning to learn that
pride was the reason of so great a fall; thus, we should
all exclaim with the prophet, "And being exalted I have

been humbled and troubled," *(Psalm 87 [88])* and say to ourselves the words which he said to Lucifer after he had mediated in his heart: "I will ascend"—"How art thou fallen from heaven, O Lucifer" *(Isaiah 14)*.

The soul is humbled according to the measure of its self-exaltation, and great must have been the pride which was followed by such a tremendous and abominable humiliation. Ah, how much more precious is one degree of humility in comparison with a thousand revelations or ecstasies!

It is a wise and just disposition of God to permit the fall of the proud into every sin and especially into that of wantonness, as being the most degrading, so that by so great a fall he should be ashamed, humbled and cured of his pride. So rightly does St. Thomas say that: "He who is fettered by pride and does not know it, falls into the sin of impurity which is manifestly of itself disgraceful, that through this sin he may rise humiliated from his confession" *(II IIæ q. 156, art. 6 ad 3)*.

MEDITATION 14

*When St. Camillus de Lellis saw the graves of the dead,
he said within himself: If these return to life, what would
they not do for eternal glory? And what do I do for my
soul, who have time? This the Saint said through humility.
But my brother, you, perhaps, have reason to fear that you
are the fruitless fig-tree of which the Lord said: Behold, for
these three years I come seeking fruit on this fig-tree, and
I find none (Luke, xiii, 7) You have been in this world for
more than three years; what fruit have you produced?*

–St. Alphonsus Liguori

❧ † ❧

However much our Christian self-love desires to avoid the remorse and repentance which ever follows the humiliations caused by sin, we should nevertheless desire and seek to be humble, because if we are humble we can never be humbled. "O my soul," we must say to ourselves, "look well into yourself and be humble if you do not want God to humble you with temporal and eternal shame." God promises to exalt the humble, and heaven is filled with the humble. God also threatens the proud with humiliation, and hell is filled with the proud. God thus promises and menaces so that if we do not remain in humility allured by His great promises, we should at least

33

remain in humility from fear of His potent threats: "And whosoever shall exalt himself shall be humbled and he that shall humble himself shall be exalted" *(Matthew 23:12).*

God regards the petitions of the humble favorably, and inclines to answer them: "He hath regard to the prayer of the humble, and He hath not despised their petition" *(Psalm 101 [102]:12).* But however much the proud man may invoke God, God will give him no spiritual consolation.

These things are all old and repeated very often, but that is because we know them and do not practice them; thus we deserve the reproof given by the prophet Daniel to Nebuchadnezzar: "Thou hast not humbled thy heart, whereas thou knewest all these things" *(Daniel 5:22).*

MEDITATION 15

Why be proud, you who are but dust and ashes?
Today here, tomorrow gone! In good health today,
a mass of ailments tomorrow! Wise today, possibly
an idiot tomorrow! Rich and rich in virtue as you
read these lines, tomorrow it may easily be said that
you find yourself a miserable wretched beggar! Show
me the Christian who will dare to extol himself when
he realizes that he is hemmed in on all sides by
so many miseries and possible misfortunes!

—St. Bonaventure

❧ † ❧

One way in which we can sin in our actions by pride is when, knowing and admitting that we have received such and such a gift of God, we nevertheless attribute it inwardly to our own merit and desire that others should do so likewise, and in our exterior demeanor we behave as if we had indeed deserved to receive these gifts. It was thus that Lucifer sinned through pride; for being infatuated with his own beauty and nobility, and although he recognized that God was the author of it all, he nevertheless had the presumption to think that he had merited it himself and was worthy to sit beside God in the highest Heaven, "I will ascend into Heaven" *(Isaiah 14:13).*

35

MEDITATION 16

*To have resisted against anger, against injury, is the crown
of patience. It is a triumph over avarice to despise money.
It is the praise of faith, by trust in the future, to suffer the
adversity of the world. And he who is not haughty
in prosperity, obtains glory for his humility.*

—St. Cyprian of Carthage

ꙮ †ꙮ

There are two kinds of humiliations: those which we
seek of our own free-will, and those which proceed from the natural and temporal vicissitudes of this
life. Against the first we must be on our guard, notwithstanding the ardor with which we embrace them, for the
ever-lurking vanity of our self-love is so subtle that it seeks
even to enhance its own vain-glory while it appears to
seek the contempt of man. But if we accept the other
humiliations which come to us, thoughts and passions
with prompt resignation to the will of God, it is a sign
of a true and sincere humility; because such humiliations
tend to mortify our self-love and to perfect the submission
which we owe to God.

Voluntary and self-sought humiliations may cause the
soul to become hypocritical. But involuntary humiliations sent to us by the Divine Will, and borne by us with

patience, sanctify the soul; and for this reason the Holy Spirit has given us this most important mandate: "In thy humiliation keep patience. For gold and silver are tried in the fire, but acceptable men in the furnace of humiliation" *(Sirach 2:4-5)*. It is impossible except in rare cases not to discover the hypocrisy of affected humility: "Touch the mountains, and they shall smoke" *(Psalm 143 [144]:5)*. And again, it is impossible not to know the virtue of true humility, because its spirit is "gentle, kind, steadfast, assured, secure, having all power" *(Wisdom 7:23)*.

MEDITATION 17

*The just man who is truly humble thinks himself
worse because he fears lest in that which he seems
to do well he should grievously sin by pride.*

—*St. Thomas Aquinas*

❧ † ❧

God resists the proud, because the proud oppose Him;
but he dispenses His graces liberally to the humble,
because they live in subjection to His will. Oh, if we humbly made place for the divine gifts, how great would be the
affluence of that grace in our souls! One of the worst consequences of our lack of humility will be that it will render
the Day of Judgement so terrible to us; because on that day
we shall not only have to give account of the graces which
we have received and of which we have made a bad use,
but also of those graces which God would have given us
if we had been humble, and which He withheld from us
on account of our pride.

It will be useless then to excuse ourselves by saying
that we fell into such and such a sin from want of grace.
"Grace was there," the Lord will answer, "but you ought to
have asked for it with humility and not forfeited it by your
pride." Pride is an obstacle harder than steel which hinders the beneficent infusion of grace into the soul. Do you
desire grace in this world and glory in the next? Humble

yourself; God created out of nothing all that we can see in our world when "the earth was void and empty," *(Genesis 1:2)* and He filled with oil all the empty vases with which the widow presented Eliseus: "Empty vessels not a few" *(4 Kings 4:3, [2 Kings])*. And He also fills with His grace those hearts which are emptied of self—that is to say, which have neither self-esteem nor self-confidence and do not rely upon their own strength.

It is most humiliating to reflect upon this, that even though we be exempt from grave sins, yet through some secret disorder within us we may be as guilty as if we had committed them. For if pride arises in our hearts and leads us to consider ourselves better than those who have committed these sins we are at once rendered guilty and worse than they in the eyes of God, because, as the Holy Spirit says, "Pride is hateful before God" *(Sirach 10:7)*.

Do not let me be dominated by pride, which is the sum of all wickedness; from my secret sins cleanse me. Purify me from those sins of pride for which I am ignorant, "then shall I be without spot" *(Psalm 18:14)*.

MEDITATION 18

But we shall certainly not be suffered to do this, nor even
to remain under the rule of a system, unless the virtue
of patience, which can only spring from humility as its
source, is first securely fixed and established in us. For
the one teaches us not to trouble any one else; the other,
to endure with magnanimity wrongs offered to us.

—St. John Cassian

✿ ✝ ✿

There are two special virtues which the Son of God
wished to teach us, and recommended us most earnestly to practice—humility and brotherly love; and it is
precisely against these two virtues that the devil wages war
the most. But it is enough that he should succeed in conquering humility for love to be overcome at the same time.

Pride is always ready to take offence; and with this
disposition to resent slights and injuries how is it possible to live in charity? When we find two people who are
prone to disagree, and to whom reconciliation is difficult,
we cannot be far wrong in concluding that both are full
of pride. Therefore, it is obvious that charity cannot exist
without humility.

Let us accept the apostolic admonition, and do not
let us blame others for their pride when they cause us

displeasure, but rather blame ourselves for not knowing how to bear that displeasure with humility. Let us begin by acquiring that patient humility ourselves which we desire so much to see in others, remembering that it is not through the patience and humility of others that we shall be saved but by our own.

MEDITATION 19

*It is no great thing for a man to be humble in abjection,
but for one who is honored, humility is altogether
a great and rare virtue.*

—*St. Bernard of Clairvaux*

❧ † ❧

It is difficult for those who possess riches or learning to
be humble, because these two gifts are apt to cause vanity in those who possess them. It is far better therefore to
be humble, than to possess great riches or great learning
and to be proud.

Nevertheless, many who are now saints in heaven
were both rich and learned when they were on earth; but
they are saints because they were humble; and both riches
and learning must be regarded as vanity, and not esteemed
except insofar as they can help us to gain eternal happiness. This is the way of the truly humble: he does not
esteem himself for his possessions or for his knowledge,
but regards these all as nothing, because he regards himself also as nothingness.

It is a beautiful sight for men and for angels to see a
rich man who is modest and apparently forgetful of his
wealth, and a wise man who seems unaware of his great
knowledge.

MEDITATION 20

When you hear evil of any one, cast any doubt you fairly can upon the accusation; or if that is impossible, make any available excuse for the culprit; and where even that may not be, be yet pitiful and compassionate, and remind those with whom you are speaking that such as stand upright do so solely through God's Grace.

—St. Francis de Sales

❧ † ❧

However upright we may be, we must never be scandalized nor amazed at the conduct of evil-doers, nor consider ourselves better than they, because we do not know what is ordained for them or for us in the supreme dispositions of God, "Who doth great things and unsearchable and wonderful things without number" *(Job 5:9)*.

When Zacchaeus though only of usury and oppressing the poor, when Magdalen filled Jerusalem with scandal, when Paul cursed and persecuted the Christian religion, who would have imagined that they would ever have become saints? And on the other hand, who would have believed that Solomon, the oracle of divine wisdom, would die in the midst of wantonness and idols? that Judas, one of the Apostles, would betray his divine Master and then give himself up to despair? Or that many holy men advanced in sanctity would have become apostates? These are examples

45

which should make us tremble when we reflect upon the unfathomable mystery of the judgement and mercy of God: "One he putteth down, and another he lifteth up" *(Psalm 74 [75]: 8)*. "He hath put down the mighty from their seat, and hath exalted the humble" *(Luke 1:52)*.

Every Saint can in a moment become a sinner if he is vain of his sanctity; and a sinner can as quickly become a Saint if he is contrite and humbles himself for his sin. How many there are who in the fervor of their prayer "mount up to the heavens" and soon afterwards, at the slightest occasion of sin, they "go down to the depths!" *(Psalm 106[107]:26)*. How many there are too who, given up to vanity and stained with the deepest sins, are suddenly changed by having their eyes opened to the knowledge of the truth and who thus attain to Christian perfection! Certainly, the high counsels of God are to be adored and not scrutinized, for "The Lord humbleth and exalteth; He raiseth up the needy from the dust, and lifteth up the poor from the dung-hill" *(1 Kings 2:7-8 [1 Samuel])*.

MEDITATION 21

But nothing can show the value which God sets on the souls of men more clearly than what the Incarnate Word has done for their redemption from sin and hell. "If," says St. Eucharius, "you do not believe your Creator, ask your Redeemer, how precious you are." Speaking of the care which we ought to have of our brethren, St. Ambrose says: "The great value of the salvation of a brother is known from the death of Christ." We judge of the value of everything by the price paid for it by an intelligent purchaser.

—St. Alphonsus Liguori

☙ † ❧

Who knows if the one I judge and speak ill of may not be dearer to God than I am? Whether another whom I esteem but little and despise for his physical or moral defects be not destined to be very happy with God for all eternity? Who knows whether I may not be condemned to the pains of hell for all eternity? With this uncertainty how can I then presume to consider myself better than any other?

No one is worth more than what he is worth in the eyes of God, and how can I know whether I am an object of hatred or of love to God? How do I know if God will fashion a vessel of honor or of dishonor from the clay of which I am made? I should thus fear, what shall I say of myself, who am so contemptible? At the day of judgment how many shall we see on the right hand of God whom we looked upon as castaways! and how many shall we see on His left whom we believed to be amongst His elect!

MEDITATION 22

*Our Creator does not wish that men should die at a
certain known time, lest during all the period before
this they should indulge in sin, and then endeavor
to be converted to God a little before their death.*

*Divine Providence hath, therefore, so disposed things
that nothing is more uncertain than the hour of death:
some die in the womb, some when scarcely born, some in
extreme old age, some in the flower of youth, whilst others
languish a long time, or die suddenly, or recover from a
severe sickness and almost incurable disease; others are
only slightly affected, but when they seem secure from
death, the disease comes on again, and takes them away.*

—St. Robert Bellarmine

⚜ † ⚜

Who can assure me that before long I shall not fall
into some mortal sin? And having once fallen, who
can assure me that I may not die in sin, and thus be condemned to eternal punishment? As long as I live in this
world I cannot be sure of anything. I must hope to save
my soul, but I must also fear to lose it. O my soul, I do not
intend to depress you; no, nor do I wish to fill you with
cowardly despair by these thoughts. I only desire you to
be humble. And how much reason do you have to humble

yourself in this uncertainty, not knowing what manner of death you shall have, or what shall be your lot for all eternity? It is only by the measure of your humility that you could hope to please God and save yourself, because it is certain that God will save "he humble people," *(Psalm 17[18]:28)* and "the humble of spirit" *(Psalm 33[34]:19).*

There are some who think that to meditate on the mystery of predestination is likely to fill us with despair; but it appears to me that this thought is a most efficacious means of practicing humility, because when I meditate upon my eternal salvation I see that it does not depend upon the power of my own free-will, but only upon the divine mercy. To not trust in myself, but place all my hope in God, so that I might say with Judith: "And let us humble our souls before Him, and continuing in a humble spirit in His service, ask the Lord that He would show His mercy to us" *(Judith 8:16-17).*

MEDITATION 23

Not only does the Lord forbid us to seek supremacy,
but would lead His hearer to the very opposite;
"He that is greatest among you shall be your servant."

—St. John Chrysostom

❧ † ❧

It is necessary, if we are to acquire humility, to be prudent in not speaking well of ourselves. "Let another praise thee," says sacred Scripture, "and not your own mouth, a stranger and not thy own lips" *(Proverbs 27:11)*.

It is very easy for us to fall into this fault of praising ourselves until it becomes a habit, and with this habit so opposed to humility how can we be humble?

What good qualities have we of our own for which we can praise ourselves? All the good that is in us comes from God, and to Him alone we must give praise and honor. When we praise ourselves we are usurping glory which is due to God alone. Even though in praising ourselves we sometimes refer all to the honor of God, it matters little; when there is no absolute necessity it is better to abstain from self-praise, for although we refer all to the glory of God with our lips, our ingenious and subtle self-love cannot fail to appropriate it secretly. And even speaking depreciatingly of ourselves there may lurk some hypocritical pride in our words, such as was mentioned by the sage of old when he said: "here is one that hum-bleth himself wickedly, and his interior is full of deceit" *(Sirach 19:23)*.

We can never watch ourselves enough, because there is nothing that teaches us so well to know the pride of our heart as our words, with which we either reveal or hide the depravity of our affections.

MEDITATION 24

*The wise of the world know how to acquire wealth,
to indulge in amusements, to gain posts of honor; yet they
do not know how to save their souls. The rich glutton
knew how to lay up wealth; but he died and was buried
in hell (Luke 16:22). Alexander the Great knew how
to acquire many kingdoms; but in a few years he died,
and was lost forever. Henry VIII knew how to preserve
his throne by rebelling against the Church; but seeing
at death that he lost his soul, he exclaimed: "We have
lost all." How many miserable sinners now weep and
cry out in hell: What has pride profited us?*

—St. Alphonsus Liguori

※ † ❧

God has Himself given us the means of obtaining this
humility of heart, in the remembrance of death and
by meditation upon it. Death is the best teacher of truth;
and pride—being nothing but an illusion of our heart—
clings to a vanity which it does not recognize as vanity;
and therefore death is the best means by which we can
learn what vanity is and how to detach our hearts from it.

Our self-love is wounded at the thought that we must
soon die, and when we least expect it, and that with death
everything comes to an end for us in this world; but at the

same time this reflection weakens the humbles of our self-love. Unfortunately, we do not think of death with that seriousness which we ought to give to it.

If a man knew for certain that he would die within a year, would he not grow more humble from day to day at the thought that each day was bringing him closer to death? But who can assure him that he ahs one year to live—when he is not certain to live to the end of the day?

O my God, true light of my soul, keep alive within me the remembrance of my death. Tell me often with Your own voice in my heart that I must die, perhaps within a year, perhaps within a month, perhaps within a week; and thus I shall remain humble. In order that the thought of death may not be unfruitful to me, excite within my soul now that knowledge and those feelings which I shall have at the last hour of my life when the blessed taper is placed in my hand "in the day of trial" *(Wisdom 3:18)*. Make me know now as I shall know then what vanity is, and then how can I ever be arrogant again in the face of that most certain truth?

MEDITATION 25

In all things consider the end; how you shall stand before
the strict Judge from Whom nothing is hidden and Who
will pronounce judgment in all justice, accepting neither
bribes nor excuses. And you, miserable sinner, what answer
will you make to the God Who knows all your sins?...
For a man will be more grievously punished in the
things in which he has sinned... the proud
will be faced with every confusion.

—Thomas à Kempis

⚘ † ⚘

Another humiliating thought lies in the remembrance of the judgement to come. Saints tremble at
the thought that they will be judged by a God in whose
presence not even the angels are immaculate. They tremble, although they have nothing to be judged except their
good works. And what will become of me, therefore, who
am guilty of so many sins?

Therefore, if I esteem myself and seek to be esteemed
by others either as more virtuous or less sinful than I really
am, it is certain that such a desire can only arise from my
own hypocrisy, by which I appear before the eyes of men
under a false disguise, leading them to believe that I am
one thing when I am really another, because I know that

they cannot see what is going on in my heart. Yet, the time will come when God will reveal my wickedness to the whole world: "I will show thy nakedness to the nations, and thy shame to kingdoms" *(Nahum 3:5)*. And then I shall appear as I really am. And what will they say of me who have been deceived by my false deceptions?

O my soul, be humble and do not forget that the more you are exalted in your own reckoning the more will you be shamed and confounded the judgement day. "Behold I come against thee, O proud one, saith the Lord, for thy day is come, the time of thy visitation. And the proud one shall fall, he shall fall down and there shall be none to lift him up" *(Isaiah 50:31)*.

MEDITATION 26

If you knew what is meant by eternity, you would easily conceive how a thousand years, compared with it, are but a moment. If an angel said to one of the damned: You will leave hell, but only after the lapse of as many ages as there are drops of water in the ocean, leaves on the trees, or grains of sand in the sea; he would feel greater joy than a beggar would at hearing of his elevation to a throne. Yes; all these ages will pass away, they will be multiplied an infinite number of times, and hell will be at its beginnings.

—St. Alphonsus Liguori

❧ † ☙

O my soul, humble yourself in in the remembrance that there is a hell, not considering it only in the abstract, nor even as a contrivance for the punishment of sinners in general, but regard it rather as a place specially prepared for you, which you have deserved more than once!

For there, the proud will be cast headlong, and I should be there with them at this moment, eternally insulted and tormented by devils, had I not been preserved from it by the mercy of God. Millions of angels have been imprisoned there for having committed one sole sin of pride and that only in thought. O my soul, if you continue in your pride and false self-esteem, guarding your own susceptibilities and oblivious of the rights of others, and "you shall be brought down to hell;" that place of torment awaits you, and there below your pride will indeed be humbled. You, who now delight in your own proud thoughts shalt there be thrust into flames of fire, and you, who now wants to be above all will then be below all. There, below you will have to face a God who bears an infinite hatred to the proud and is infinitely angry with them. And as it is a truth that the humble shall be exalted in heaven, it is also a truth that the proud shall be humbled and cast down into hell.

"And the rich man also died;" as St. Luke writes of the proud man who was "clothed in purple and fine linen." And the rich man died—that is the end of al humanity and vanity; and "he was buried in hell" *(Luke 16:22)* —that is the end of all pride. The grave is the end of man; hell is the end of the proud.

MEDITATION 27

We have lived in the discipline a long time: but rather as though making a beginning daily let us increase our earnestness. For the whole life of man is very short, measured by the ages to come, wherefore all our time is nothing compared with eternal life.

—St. Anthony of the Desert

༄ † ༄

Above all, the thought of eternity should keep us humble. Taking it for granted that I am mistaken in practicing humility in this world, and in giving place to others, I know that my mistake is small because everything below comes quickly to an end; but if I am deceiving myself by living in reckless pride, my mistake is great because it will last for all eternity. Even if I were living in humility, I should still fear because I can never be sure whether this humility which I think I possess is true humility or not; how much more then should I fear because I can never be sure whether this humility which I think I possess is true humility or not; how much more then, should I fear if I am living in open pride?

On this side of the grave all things pass away, but on the other side what will become of me? To this I give no thought; and to speak the truth this is the reason why I am dominated by vanity, because I give so little thought to eternity. King David was most humble of heart because he was filled with the dread of eternity: "And I meditate in the night with my own heart: Will God then cast off forever" *(Psalm 76 [77]:7-8).*

How many of those who were conspicuous among the proud of this world have overcome their pride and acquired humility by one single serious thought of eternity! The words of the prophet have always been and will always be found true: "And the ancient mountains were crushed to pieces, the hills of the world were bowed down by the journeys of His eternity" *(Habakkuk 3:6).*

MEDITATION 28

Jesus says "humble of heart," but was He not also humble of mind? Although He was without sin, he humbled Himself like a sinner. He had nothing to be ashamed of. As the good thief put it: "This man has done no wrong." But we have done everything to be ashamed of.

—St. Peter Julian Eymard

❧ † ☙

I am poor in soul, without virtue or merit, full of iniquity and malice, and yet I esteem myself and love my own esteem so much that I am troubled if others do not esteem me also. I am truly a poor, proud, miserable creature; and the greater my poverty, the more my pride is detestable in the eyes of God. All this proceeds from not knowing myself. Grant, O my God, that I may say with the prophet: "I am the man that see my poverty" *(Lamentations 3:1)*. Make known unto me, O Lord, mine own wretchedness, that of myself I am nothing, know nothing, and possess nothing but my sins, and deserve nothing but Hell. I have received many graces from You, as well as lights and inspirations, and much help, and yet with what ingratitude have I responded to Your infinite goodness! Who is more sinful, more ungrateful, and more wicked than I? The more You have done for me, the humbler I ought to be, for I shall have to render unto You a most strict account of all Your benefits: "And unto whomsoever much is given, of him much shall be required" *(Luke 12:48)*. And yet the greater Your goodness, the greater my pride. I blush with shame, and it is the knowledge of my pride that obliges me now to be humble.

MEDITATION 29

*I say the same of humility and of all the virtues;
the wiles of the devil are terrible, he will run a thousand
times round hell if by so doing he can make us believe
that we have a single virtue which we have not. And he is
right, for such ideas are very harmful, and such imaginary
virtues, when they come from this source, are never unac-
companied by vainglory; just as those which God
gives are free both from this and from pride.*

–St. Teresa of Ávila

❧ † ❧

We must not be too apt to flatter ourselves that we
possess any special virtue. Our chastity may be the
result of a want of opportunities or temptations: and in like
manner our patience may proceed from a phlegmatic temperament, or be dictated by worldly, and not by Christian,
wisdom. This can be said of many other virtues in which
we are liable to make the same mistake.

We must study this doctrine well, that the true Christian virtues are "born not of blood, nor of the will of the
flesh, nor of the will of man, but of God;" *(John 1:13)* that
is, that they are not the work either of the desires, passions
or reason of man, but proceed from God as their first prin-
ciple, and return to God as their last end. This knowledge

is necessary for us, so that we may not imagine ourselves to be virtuous when we are not, nor think ourselves better than others when we see them falling into some sin.

We should ever learn lessons of humility from the faults of others, and say: If I had found myself in like circumstances, and had had the same temptation, perhaps I should have done worse. If God does not permit great temptations to assail me, it is because He knows my weakness and that I should succumb to them; with eyes of compassion He sees what I am, "a weak man" *(Wisdom 9:5).* And if I do not fall into sin, it is not by my own virtue, but by God's grace. Let me therefore abide in humility, and it is to my advantage, because if in my pride I count myself greater than others, God will abandon me and suffer me to fall, and will humble me through those very things for which I wish to exalt myself.

MEDITATION 30

*What greater destiny can befall man's humility than
that he should be intermingled with God, and by this
intermingling should be deified, and that we should
be so visited by the Dayspring from on high, that even
that Holy Thing that should be born should be called the
Son of the Highest, and that there should be bestowed
upon Him a Name which is above every name?
And what else can this be than God?*

—St. Gregory Nazianzen

☙ † ❧

As Paradise is only for the humble, therefore in Paradise everyone will have more or less glory according
to his degree of humility. God has exalted Jesus Christ in
glory above all, because He was the humblest of all: being
the true Son of God He yet elected to become the most
abject of all men. And after Jesus Christ the most exalted
of all was His holy Mother, because being superior to all
in her dignity as Mother of God she yet humbled herself
more than all by her profound humility. This rule, dictated
by the wisdom of God, applies to all the other Saints who
are exalted in their glory in Heaven in proportion to their
humility on earth.

Scripture says that "Humility goeth before glory" *(Proverbs 15:33)*. Job had said the same: "For he that hath been humbled shall be in glory" *(Job 22:29)*. But the Savior of the world spoke more plainly still when, having shown that humility was necessary to enter the kingdom of Heaven, He called a little child to Himself, and said: "Whosoever therefore shall humble himself as this little child, he is the greater in the kingdom of Heaven" *(Matthew 18:4)*. And, how precious humility must be when God recompenses it with eternal glory! Oh, my soul, lift up the eyes of thy faith to Paradise, and consider whether it be not best to be humble in our short existence here on earth, so as to enter with joy into the immeasurable glory of that happy eternity? "For that which is at present momentary, worketh for us above measure exceedingly an eternal weight of glory" *(1 Corinthians 4:17)*. Recommend thyself with all thy heart to that God, "Who setteth up the humble on high" *(Job 5:11)*.

MEDITATION 31

*The treasure hidden in the field is the desire of heaven;
the field in which the treasure is hidden is the discipline
of heavenly learning; this, when a man finds, he hides,
in order that he may preserve it; for zeal and affections
heavenward it is not enough that we protect from evil
spirits, if we do not protect from, human praises. For in
this present life we are in the way which leads to our
country, and evil spirits as robbers beset us in our journey.
Those therefore who carry their treasure openly, they seek
to plunder in the way. When I say this, I do not mean
that our neighbors should not see our works, but that in
what we do, we should not seek praise from without. The
kingdom of heaven is therefore compared to things of earth,
that the mind may rise from things familiar to things
unknown, and may learn to love the unknown by
that which it knows is loved when known.*

—St. Gregory the Great

❧ † ☙

At times we are over-scrupulous about works of super-
erogation, such for instance as having omitted on
such a day to say a certain prayer or to perform some
self-imposed mortification; these are scruples of omissions
which in regard to our eternal salvation are of little or no

importance; but we take but little heed of that humility which is to us most essential and necessary and without which no one can be saved. St. Paul warns us: "Do not become children in sense" *(1 Corinthians 14:20)*. Do not be like children who cry and despair if an apple is taken away from them, but care little for losing a gem of great value. Let us place humility above all things. It is the hidden treasure buried in the field, to acquire which we ought to sell all we possess *(Matthew 13:44)*.

Do not let us call these sins against humility scruples, but let us regard them as real sins, worthy of confession and of amendment. May God guard us from too easy a conscience in respect to that true humility which is commanded us in the Gospel. We should indeed be taking the broad way mentioned by the Holy Spirit, which, though it seems the right and straight road nevertheless leads direct to perdition: "There is a way that seemeth to a man right, and the ends thereof lead to death" *(Proverbs 16:25)*.

There are people who think like the Pharisees that virtue and sanctity consist in prayers of great length, in the visiting of churches, and in some special abstinence, in retreats, in modesty of attire, in spiritual conferences or in some exercise of exterior piety; but in all this who thinks of humility? Who esteems it and studies to acquire it? What is all this then but a vain delusion?

MEDITATION 32

It appears to me that humility is the truth.
I know not whether I am humble, but I know
that I see the truth in all things.

—St. Thérèse of Lisieux

☙ † ❧

The heart of the proud man is like a stormy sea, never at rest, while the heart of the humble is fully content in its humility—"Rich in his being low" *(James 1:10)*—and is always calm and tranquil and without fear that anything in this world should disturb him, and shall "rest with confidence" *(Isaiah 14:30)*. And from whence proceeds this difference? The humble man enjoys peace and quiet because he lives according to the rules of truth and justice, submitting his own will in all things to the Divine will. The proud man is always agitated and perturbed because of the opposition he is continually offering to the Divine will in order to fulfill his own.

The more the heart is filled with self-love, so much the greater will be its anxiety and agitation. This maxim is indeed true; for whenever I feel myself inwardly irritated, disturbed and angered by some adversity which has befallen me, I need not look elsewhere for the cause of such feelings than within myself, and I should always do well to say: If I were truly humble I should not be disquieted. My great agitation is an evident proof which ought to convince me that my self-love is great and dominant and powerful within me, and is the tyrant which torments and gives me no peace.

If I feel aggrieved by some sharp word that has been said to me, or by some discourtesy shown me, from whence does this feeling of pain proceed? From my pride alone. Oh, if I were truly humble, what calm, what peace and happiness would my soul not enjoy! And this promise of Jesus Christ is infallible: "Learn of Me, because I am meek and humble of heart, and you shall find rest to your souls" *(Matthew 11:29).*

MEDITATION 33

Some persons do not love tribulation, but only the
honor which attends it. A really patient servant of God
is as ready to bear inglorious troubles as those which are
honorable. A brave man can easily bear with contempt,
slander and false accusation from an evil world; but
to bear such injustice at the hands of good men,
of friends and relations, is a great test of patience.

—St. Francis de Sales

❧ † ☙

The proof of true humility is patience: neither meekness of speech, nor humbleness of bearing, nor the giving up of oneself to lowly works, are sufficient indications by which to judge if a soul is truly humble. There are many who bear all the appearance of exterior humility, but who are angered at every slight adversity, and resent any little vexation which they may encounter.

If under certain circumstances we show toleration and patience in bearing an insult, in suffering a wrong in silence without indignation and anger or resentment, it is a good sign, and we may begin to conclude that we have some humility; but even then patience can only be an infallible sign of true humility when it proceeds from the recognition of our own unworthiness and when we tolerate the wrong because we know that we ourselves are full of faults and are deserving of it.

And how do we stand in regard to this patience, O my soul? O my God, how much pride I find even in my patience! Sometimes I suffer a wrong, but at the same time I feel that I am wronged. I suffer an insult, but consider that I do not deserve it: and if others do not esteem me, yet I esteem myself. Is there humility here? Not a shred of it!

MEDITATION 34

We must unite ourselves to God's will not only in things that come to us directly from his hands, such as sickness, desolation, poverty, death of relatives, but likewise in those we suffer from man—for example, contempt, injustice, loss of reputation, loss of temporal goods and all kinds of persecution. On these occasions we must remember that whilst God does not will the sin, he does will our humiliation, our poverty, or our mortification, as the case may be.

—St. Alphonsus Liguori

�֍ † ֎

I ought to be most grateful to anyone who helps to keep me in humility by subjecting me to humiliations of word and deed, because he is co-operating with the Divine mercy to fulfill the work of my eternal salvation. And although he has no thought of my salvation when he offends me, he is nevertheless an instrument thereof, and all the evil comes from me if I do not make a good use of it. We are grateful to the surgeon who bleeds us, even though he may not be thinking of our health but of this particular office of his profession. Therefore, if we understood this, not as Stoic philosophers but as good Christians, we ought to be grateful to those who humiliate us, for although they have no intention of making us humble but only of humiliating us, yet in reality this humiliation helps us to acquire humility if such be our desire.

MEDITATION 35

Earthly riches are like the reed. Its roots are sunk in the
swamp, and its exterior is fair to behold; but inside it is
hollow. If a man leans on such a reed, it will snap off and
pierce his soul, and his soul will be carried off to hell.

–St. Anthony of Padua

When I consider the words which Jesus Christ addressed to His heavenly Father in prayer, saying that He did not pray for the world, *(John 18:9)*—and again that, when praying for His disciples that His prayer might be more efficacious, He emphasized the fact that they were not followers of the world, I confess that no words of our Saviour in the whole Gospel terrify me more than these. For I perceive that it is necessary for me to separate myself from the world, so that Jesus Christ may intercede for me. And if I am a lover of the world, I shall be excommunicated by Jesus Christ and shall have no part in His intercessions and prayers. These are the words of Christ Himself: "I pray not for the world, but for those who are not of the world."

Let us really understand these words: that Jesus Christ excludes us from His kingdom if we belong to the world, that is to say if we wish to follow the maxims of the world which are nothing but vanity and deceit and fill man with pride; the maxims of the world which the prophet says "turn aside the way of the humble" *(Amos 2:7)*. Meanwhile Jesus Christ is our advocate with the Father in so far as, renewing our Baptismal vow, we renounce the world and accept the maxims of the Gospel which are true and tend to make man humble. To serve both God and the world is impossible, because we could never please both—"he will hold to the one and despise the other" *(Luke 16: 13)*.

To pretend to serve God and the world is the same as to imagine that we can be both humble and proud at the same time. Vain dream!

MEDITATION 36

Let us detach ourselves in spirit from all that we see and cling to that which we believe. This is the cross which we must imprint on all our daily actions and behavior.

—St. Peter Damian

≫ † ≪

The most familiar meditation which the seraphic St. Francis was in the habit of making was this, first he elevated his thoughts to God and then turned them towards himself: "My God," he would exclaim, "Who art Thou? and who am I?" And raising his thoughts first to the greatness and infinite goodness of God he would then descend to consider his own misery and vileness. And thus ascending and descending this scale of thought from the greatness of God down to his own nothingness the seraphic Saint would pass whole nights in meditation, practicing in this exercise a real, true, sublime and profound humility, like the Angels seen by Jacob in his sleep on that ladder of mystical perfection "ascending and descending by it" *(Genesis 18:12)*.

This should be our model that we may not err in the exercise of humility. To fix our thoughts solely on our own wretchedness might cause us to fall into self-distrust and despair, and in the same way to fix our thoughts solely on the contemplation of the Divine goodness might cause us to be presumptuous and rash.

Distrust yourself and confide in God, and thus distrusting and thus confiding, between fear and hope, you shall work out your salvation in the spirit of the Gospel.

MEDITATION 37

And let not the worshipper, beloved brethren, be ignorant
in what manner the publican prayed with the Pharisee
in the temple. Not with eyes lifted up boldly to heaven,
nor with hands proudly raised; but beating his breast,
and testifying to the sins shut up within, he
implored the help of the divine mercy.

—St. Cyprian of Carthage

꙳ † ꙳

Self-knowledge is a great help for acquiring humility;
but in the midst of the many passions, faults and vices
of which we are aware, to recognize our own pride is the
most useful of all. For this vice is the most shameful of all,
and even in our confessions it is more difficult for us to say
truthfully: "I accuse myself of being proud and of not trying seriously to correct this fault" than to accuse ourselves
of many other sins. This knowledge of our pride is most
humiliating; for where certain other vices may be pitied
and excused for some reason or other, pride can never be
pitied or excused, being a sin which is diabolical and odious not only to God but to men—as the inspired word
says: "Pride is hateful before God and men" *(Sirach 10:7).*

Let us therefore examine ourselves daily on this
point; let us accuse ourselves of it in our confessions;
and acknowledging our pride in this manner will be an

excellent incentive to become humble. Let us pray to Jesus Christ that He may do for us as He did for the blind man whom He healed, and ask Him to put the mud of pride upon our eyes so that we may be made to see. Let us say to God: "Thou art my God, that God Who raiseth up the needy from the earth and lifteth up the poor out of the dunghill," *(Psalm 112 [113]:7)* grant that this pride which is my great sin may through Thee serve as an instrument by which I may attain to a virtuous humility!

MEDITATION 38

Pride only, the chief of all iniquities, can make us treat gifts as if they were rightful attributes of our nature, and, while receiving benefits, rob our Benefactor of His due glory.

—*St. Bernard of Clarivaux*

†

L et us consider the things of this world in which we are apt to take a vain delight. One may pride himself on his robust health and bodily strength, another on the science, knowledge, eloquence and other gifts that he has acquired through study and art. Another prides himself upon his wealth and possessions; another upon his nobility and rank; another upon his moral virtues, or other virtues which bring him spiritual grace and perfection: but must not all these gifts be regarded as so many benefits proceeding from God, for which we must render an account if we do not use them to resist temptation and conform to the ordination of God? We are debtors to God for every benefit that we receive, and are bound to employ these gifts and to trade with them for the glory of God like merchants to whom capital is entrusted. When we consider how many benefits, both of body and soul, we have received from Him, we are compelled to admit that there are so many debts which we have contracted towards Him, and why should we glory in our debts?

No prudent merchant, if he has large debts, would go and proclaim the fact in the marketplace and thereby lose his credit; and how can we expect to gain credit by boasting of the many debts we owe to God? Debts so heavy that we run the risk of becoming bankrupt on that day when our Lord and Master will say: "Pay what thou owest" *(Matthew 8:28).*

MEDITATION 39

Some men become indignant when others do not esteem
their spiritual practices. This arises from secret self-esteem
and pride, and they can never quite realize that they are
steeped in pride up to their very eyes. For they think that
a certain degree of recognition of their own wretchedness
suffices, and, although they have this, they are full of secret
self-esteem and self-satisfaction, taking more delight in
their own spirituality and spiritual gifts than in those
of others. They are like the Pharisee who gave thanks to
God that he was not as other men, and that he practiced
such and such virtues, whereat he was satisfied
with himself and presumed thereon.

—St. John of the Cross

❧ † ☙

To give thanks to God for all the blessings we have received and are continually receiving is an excellent means of exercising humility, because by thanksgiving we learn to acknowledge the Supreme Giver of every good: and for this reason it is necessary for us always to be humble before God. St. Paul exhorts us to render thanks for all things and at all times: "In all things give thanks" *(1 Thessalonians 5:18)* "Giving thanks always for all things" *(Ephesians 5:20).* But that our thanksgiving may be an act of humility it must not only come from the lips but from the heart with a firm conviction that all good comes to us through the infinite mercy of God. Look at a beggar who has received a considerable gift from a rich man, with what warmth he expresses his gratitude! He is astonished that the rich man should have deigned to bestow a gift upon him, protesting that he is unworthy of it, and that he receives it, not through his own merit, but through the noble kindness of the giver, to whom he will always be most grateful. He speaks from his heart because he knows his own miserable condition of poverty and the benign condescension of the rich man. And should the thanks we give to God be less than the thanks which are given from man to man? When one man can thus thank another, ought we not to blush with shame that there should be men who feel more humility of heart towards their fellow-men than we do towards God?

MEDITATION 40

Another of Aloysius Gonzaga's privileges was to be free
of all distractions in his prayers, and how great a privilege
that was, we who try to pray know best. I asked him once
how on earth he was able to so compose his mind in prayer
as to pass a whole hour without the least distraction. Do
you know what his answer was? "The real wonder, Father,
is how anybody could possibly turn his mind to other
things while standing in the presence of God."

−St. Robert Bellarmine

❧ † ☙

We often lament that we are unable to pray because
of the many distractions which hinder our recollec-
tion and dry up the source of devotion in our hearts, but in
this we err and do not know what we are saying. The best
prayer is not that in which we are most recollected and
fervent, but that in which we are most humble; because it
is written: "The prayer of him that humbleth himself shall
pierce the clouds" *(Sirach 35:21)*. And what distractions
of mind and heart can prevent our exercising humility? It
is precisely in those moments when we feel irritable and
tepid that we ought to show our humility, and how? By
saying: O Lord, I am not worthy to remain here speaking to You so confidentially, I do not deserve the grace of

prayer because it is a special gift which You have bestowed upon those dear to You. It is enough for me to be Your servant, chasing away my distractions as so many flies. For flies do not fly round boiling water, but only round tepid water, and all these distractions arise from my great tepidity. Ah, what an excellent prayer!

The more the soul exalts itself and takes pleasure in its own meditation, so much the more does God exalt Himself above that soul and remains apart from it. "Man shall come to a deep heart and God shall be exalted" *(Psalm 63 [64], 8)*. Do we desire that God in His mercy should come nigh to us? Let us humble ourselves. "Do you wish God to draw near to you?" says St. Augustine, "humble yourself, for the more you raise yourself, the more will He be above you."

MEDITATION 41

This is the beautiful freedom of the sons of God, and it is worth vastly more than all the rank and distinction of blood and birth, more than all the kingdoms in the world. This is the abiding peace which, in the experience of the saints, "surpasseth all understanding." It surpasses all pleasures rising from gratification of the senses, from social gatherings, banquets and other worldly amusements; vain and deceiving as they are, they captivate the senses for the time being, but bring no lasting contentment; rather they afflict man in the depth of his soul where alone true peace can reside.

—St. Alphonsus Liguori

❧ † ☙

Prayer, says St. Augustine, is essentially the resource of him who knows that he is both poor and needy *(Enarr. in Ps. xxvi)*. Let us acknowledge and confess our poverty and indigence before God, and by this confession we shall exercise humility. The really poor do not need to be taught how to ask alms humbly. Necessity is their master, and if man can humble himself before man, why should he not also humble himself before God?

If we wish to discern what belongs to God and that which is our own, it is sufficient for us to reflect that by rendering to God all that is His, nothing is left to ourselves but nothingness. So that we can truly say with the prophet: "I am brought to nothing" *(Psalm 72[73]:21)*. This is a true saying, that all that is within us that is more than nothingness belongs to God, and He can take away what is His when He chooses without doing us any wrong.

This reflection alone should suffice to make us humble, and it may be said that all true humility depends upon our persevering seriously in this thought. Oh, my soul, thou shalt be humbled when, as God says by the prophet, He will "separate the precious from the vile" *(Jeremiah 15:19)*. Thus the essence of humility consists in knowing how to discern rightly that which is mine, and that which belongs to God. All the good that I do comes from God, and nothing belongs to me but my own nothingness. What was I in the abyss of eternity? A mere nothing. And what did I do of myself to emerge from that nothingness? Nothing. If God had not created me, where should I be? In nothingness. If God did not uphold me at every turn, whither should I return? Into nothingness. Therefore it is clear that I possess nothing of myself but nothingness. Even in my moral being I possess nothing but my own wickedness. When I do evil it is entirely my own work, when I do good it belongs to God alone. Evil is a work of my own wickedness; good is a work of God's mercy. In this way we separate the precious from the vile; this is the art of all arts, the science of sciences, and the wisdom of the Saints.

MEDITATION 42

We must be much more ardent in bringing the inner man into subjection than in mortifying the body; in breaking the movements of the soul than in breaking bones. It is more difficult to tame the spirit than to lacerate the flesh.

—St. Ignatius of Loyola

❧ † ❧

We need not be astonished nor sad when we feel these instincts within us. They belong to the wickedness of our corrupt nature and are remnants of the temptation of our first parents by the serpent, when he said to them: "And you shall be as gods" *(Genesis 3:5)*. Therefore I repeat that these desires which arise from the weakness and depravity of our human nature must be borne with patience. If these desires gain the mastery over us, it is because we have encouraged and given way to them; and a bad habit which we have formed ourselves can only be cured by ourselves, and therefore the mortification of the same also lies with us. This mortification of the senses, inspired by humility, is taught by Christ in the self-denial which He imposed upon us when He said: "If any man will follow Me, let him deny himself" *(Matthew 16:24)*. And therefore I must draw this conclusion, that if I will not mortify myself with humility—that is to say, crush my self-love and craving for esteem—I shall be excluded as a follower of Jesus Christ, and by such an exclusion I shall also forfeit His grace and be eternally exiled from participating in His glory.

But in order to practice it, it is necessary for me to do violence to myself, as it is written: "The kingdom of heaven suffereth violence, and the violent bear it away" *(Matthew 11:12)*. Who can obtain salvation, except by doing violence to himself?

MEDITATION 43

There is then no other fault which is so destructive of all virtues, and robs and despoils a man of all righteousness and holiness, as this evil of pride, which like some pestilential disease attacks the whole man, and, not content to damage one part or one limb only, injures the entire body by its deadly influence, and endeavors to cast down by a most fatal fall, and destroy those who were already at the top of the tree of the virtues. Once it has taken possession of some unfortunate soul, like some most brutal tyrant, when the lofty citadel of the virtues has been taken, utterly destroys and lays waste the whole city; and levelling with the ground of vices the once high walls of saintliness, and confusing them together, it allows no shadow of freedom henceforth to survive in the soul subject to it.

—St. John Cassian

≈ † ≈

Let us listen at the gates of Hell and hear the lamentations of the eternally damned. They exclaim: "What hath pride profited us?" *(Wisdom 5:8).* What use or advantage was our pride to us? Everything passes and vanishes like a shadow, and of all those past evils nothing remains to us but the eternal shame of having been proud.

Their remorse is vain, because it is the remorse of despair. Therefore, while there is still time let us consider the matter seriously, and say: "What advantage have I derived from all my pride? It makes me hateful to Heaven and earth, and if I do not insist upon mortifying it, it will make me odious to myself for all eternity in Hell." Let us lift up our eyes to Heaven, and, contemplating the Saints, exclaim: "Behold how their humility has profited them! Oh, how much glory have they gained by their humility!" Now, humility is looked upon as madness by the worldly, worthy only of scorn and derision; but a time will come when they will be obliged to recognize its virtue, and to exclaim, in seeing the glory of the humble: "Behold how they are numbered among the children of God" *(Wisdom 5:5)*.

If I am humble, I shall be exalted with that glory to which God exalts the humble. O my God, humble this mad pride which predominates within me. "Thou shalt multiply strength in my soul," *(Psalm 137:3)* for, "my strength hath left me" *(Psalm 37:11)*. And I will not and cannot do anything without Your help. In You I place all my trust, and beseech You to help me. "But I am needy and poor; O God, help me. Thou art my helper and my deliverer: O Lord, make no delay" *(Psalm 69: 6)*.

MEDITATION 44

*Brother Elias ventured to present himself to him, in a
cleaner habit, and one made of finer cloth than those of
the other brethren, and he assumed an air little suitable to
his profession. Francis, dissembling what was passing in
his mind, said to him: "I beg you to lend me that habit." Elias did not dare refuse: he went aside and took it
of and brought it to him, Francis put it on over his own,
smoothed it down, and then, strutting fiercely with his
head erect, he said in a loud voice: "God preserve you,
good people." Then taking the habit off indignantly,
he threw it from him with contempt. After this he resumed
his usual demeanor and walked humbly with his old
and tattered habit, saying: "Such is the deportment
of the true Friars Minor."*

—The Life and Legends of St. Francis of Assisi

☙ ✝ ❧

If we feel inward satisfaction when we are given credit
for a humility which we do not possess, why do we not
endeavor to acquire that with which we like to be cred-
ited? If we seek after the vain shadow of humility, it means
that we care very little for the substance of this virtue. A
man who would be contented with the appearance of virtue without trying to acquire it in reality, would resemble

a merchant who valued false pearls and gems more than real ones.

O my soul, perhaps you too are among those who, being proud, resent the accusation of pride and desire to be thought humble! This would be lying to thy own conscience, lying to God, to His Angels, and to men. As St. Paul says: "We are made a spectacle to the world, and to Angels, and to men" *(1 Corinthians 4:9).*

It is a shameful thing for us to wish to appear humble when we are not so. There are certain occasions when in our interior acts we must practice humility; but we must watch over ourselves carefully, so that in thus practicing it we may not desire to be thought humble. And that is why hidden acts of humility are safer than exterior ones. But if there is pride in wishing that the humility we have should be recognized and known, what measure of presumption would there not be in wishing to be thought humble when we have no humility?

MEDITATION 45

What, on the other hand, was the lot of the Pharisee?
Here was a man praying, fasting and doing many good
works, and in spite of all that he was censured by God.
Why was this? Simply because he prided himself on
his good works and took satisfaction out of them
as though they were of his own doing.

—St. Vincent de Paul

✿ † ✿

We may persuade ourselves that we possess various
virtues, because we have a tangible proof within us
that we really have them. Thus we may judge ourselves to
be chaste, because we feel really attracted to chastity; or
we may think ourselves abstemious, because we are so by
nature; or obedient, because we practice a ready obedience. But however much a man may exercise humility, he
can never form any judgment as to his being really humble, for he who thinks himself humble is no longer so.

In the same way that to recognize that we are proud
is the beginning of humility, so to flatter ourselves that
we are humble is the beginning of pride, and the more
humble we think ourselves the greater is our pride. That
self-complacency which the heart feels, making us imagine that we are humble in consequence of some agree-
able reflections we have had about ourselves, is a species

of vanity; and how can vanity exist with humility which is founded solely on truth? Vanity is nothing but a lie, and it is precisely from a lie that pride springs.

Let us pray to God with the prophet: "Let not the foot of pride come to me" *(Psalm 35:12)*. Grant, O my God, that I may be humble, but that I may not know that I am humble. Make me holy, yet ignorant of holiness; for if I should learn to know or even to imagine myself holy, I should become vain; and through vanity should lose all humility and holiness.

MEDITATION 46

Thus, if the love of God reign within us, we will despise
ourselves: if self-love reign, we will despise God. But,
in conquering self-love consists the victory to which
shall be given a crown of eternal glory.

—St. Alphonsus Liguori

≫ † ≪

But in order to acquire humility, it is necessary also to be prudent in not speaking well of oneself. "Let. another praise thee," says the inspired word, "and not thy own mouth, a stranger and not thy own lips" *(Proverbs 27:11)*.

It is very easy for us to fall into this fault of praising ourselves until it becomes a habit, and with this habit—so opposed to humility—how can we be humble?

What good qualities have we of our own for which we can praise ourselves? All the good that is in us comes from God, and to Him alone we must give praise and honor. When, therefore, we praise ourselves we are usurping glory which is due to God alone. Even though in praising ourselves we sometimes refer all to the honor of God, it matters little; when there is no absolute necessity it is better to abstain from self-praise, for although we refer all to the glory of God with our lips, our ingenious and subtle self-love cannot fail to appropriate it secretly. And even speaking depreciatingly of ourselves there may lurk some hypocritical pride in our words, such as was mentioned by the sage of old when he said: "There is one that humbleth himself wickedly, and his interior is full of deceit" *(Sirach 19:23)*.

Therefore we can never watch over ourselves enough, because there is nothing that teaches us so well to know the pride of our heart as our words, with which we either reveal or hide the depravity of our affections. And this is the characteristic of the proud, according to St. Bernard: "One who boastfully proclaims what he is, or lies about what he is not."

Let us bear in heart and mind this precious advice given by Tobias to his son: "Never suffer pride to reign in thy mind or in thy words" *(Tobit 4:14)*. The words of a proud man are nauseous, whether he speaks of himself or others, and they are hated both by God and man: therefore we should detest this vice, not only from the Christian but also from the human standpoint.

MEDITATION 47

Be careful to give no credit to yourself for anything;
if you do, you are stealing from God, to whom
alone every good thing is due.

—St. Vincent de Paul

❧ † ☙

There is no valid excuse for not being humble, because
we have always, within and without, abundant reasons
for humility: "And thy humiliation shall be in the midst of
thee. It is the Holy Ghost who sends us this warning by
the mouth of His prophet Micheas" *(Micah 6:14).*

When we consider well what we are in body, and
what we are in soul, it seems to me most easy to humble
oneself, and even most difficult to be proud. To be humble it suffices that I should nourish within myself that
right feeling which belongs to every man who is honorable in the eyes of the world, to be content with one's
own without unjustly depriving our neighbor of what is
his. Therefore, as I have nothing of my own but my own
nothingness, it is sufficient for humility that I should be
content with this nothingness. But if I am proud, I become
like a thief, appropriating to myself that which is not mine
but God's. And most assuredly it is a greater sin to rob
God of that which belongs to God than to rob man of
that which is man's.

To be humble let us listen to the revelation of the Holy Ghost which is infallible. "Behold you are nothing, and your work is of that which hath no being" *(Isaiah 41:24)*. But who is really convinced of his own nothingness?

To know what our body is in reality, it will suffice for us to look into the grave, for, from what we see there, we must inevitably conclude that as it is with those decayed bodies, so it will soon be with us. And with this reflection I must say to myself: "Why is earth and ashes proud?" *(Sirach 10:9)*. "Behold the glory of man! for his glory is dung and worms; today he is lifted up, and tomorrow he shall not be found, because he is returned into his earth, and his thought is come to nothing" *(1 Maccabees 2:62, 63)*.

O my soul, without going further to seek truth, enter in thought into the heart of thy dwelling which is thy body!

MEDITATION 48

He who falls into sin, however light it may be, ought
to rise immediately, have recourse to God, beg pardon
of Him, and ask grace never to commit it again.

−St. Aloysius Gonzaga

❧ † ❧

Every morning we ought to make this prayer and daily
offering to God: I offer Thee, O my God, all my
thoughts, all my words and all my actions of this day. Grant
that they may be thoughts of humility, words of humility,
and actions of humility—all to Thy glory.

Also during the course of the day it will be well to
exclaim with this prayer: "Lord Jesus, give me a humble
and contrite heart." These few words contain all that we
can possibly ask of God; because in praying for a contrite
heart we ask Him for that which is necessary to ensure
forgiveness for our past life, and in praying for a humbled
heart all that which is required to secure life everlasting.
Oh, may I, at the hour of death, find myself with a contrite
and humbled heart! Then what confidence shall I not have
in the mercy of God if I can exclaim with King David:
"A contrite and humble heart, O my God, Thou wilt not
despise." We very often offer prayers to God to which He
might justly reply: "Thou knowest not what thou askest,"
but when we ask for holy humility, we know for certain

we are asking for something which is most pleasing to God and most necessary to ourselves; and in asking for this we must believe that God will maintain His infallible promise: "Ask, and it shall be given you" *(Matthew 7:7)*.

MEDITATION 49

You aspire to great things? Begin with little ones.
You desire to erect a very high building? Think first
of the foundation of humility. The higher one intends it,
the deeper must the foundation be laid.

—*St. Augustine of Hippo*

❧ † ☙

The more we reflect upon this great virtue of humility, the more we should learn to love and honor it. It is natural to the soul to love a good which it recognizes as such, and there is no doubt that we shall love humility when we recognize its intrinsic value and the good that comes of it. Our love of what is good is measured by our knowledge of it, and in the same measure that we love we desire to obtain it, and in the measure that we desire it we embrace the most proper and efficacious means of acquiring it. It was thus that the wise man acted in order to obtain wisdom. He loved her, desired and prayed for her, and applied his whole mind to possess her, so great was the esteem in which he held her: "Wherefore I wished, and understanding was given me, and I preferred her before kingdoms and thrones, and esteemed riches nothing in comparison of her" *(Wisdom 7:7)*.

It is necessary to thoroughly understand this doctrine because we shall never succeed in acquiring humility unless we really desire to obtain it; nor shall we ever desire it unless we have learnt to love it, nor shall we love it unless we have realized what humility really is—a great and most precious good, absolutely essential to our eternal welfare. Consider for a little while in what esteem you hold humility. Do you love it? Do you desire it? What do you do to acquire it? Do you ask this virtue of God in your prayers? Do you have recourse to the intercession of the Blessed Virgin? Do you willingly read those books that treat of humility, or the lives of those Saints who were most noted for their humility? Examine yourself and see whether your desire for humility be only a passing fancy, or really in your will.

MEDITATION 50

For you see your enemies are not satisfied with inflicting mortal wounds on your Body, but must scoff at your patience, and howl in triumph at your ill-treatment; you look upon them, I say, not as a foe scans his antagonists, but as a father regards his wandering children, as a doctor listens to the ravings of a delirious patient. This is why you are not angry with them but pity them, and entrust them to the care of your all-powerful Father, that He would cure them and make them whole. This is the effect of true charity, to be on good terms with all men, to consider no one your enemy, and to live at peace with those who hate peace.

—St. Robert Bellarmine

☙ † ❧

Is it not well to apply ourselves to eradicate a fault, when we know that by so doing our hearts will be gladdened? And therefore is it not true that once our pride, which is the cause of so many of our troubles, is subdued, we shall be far happier?

We feel a natural aversion towards the proud, and we cannot love them; but may not this instinct of aversion which we have towards the proud be felt by others towards ourselves? For it is true that "Pride is hurtful always" *(Sirach 10:7)*. Sometimes we lament that others do not love or esteem us. Let us examine the cause, and we shall find that it proceeds from our pride. On the other hand, do we not see the affection that is generally shown towards the humble? Every one seeks their company, everyone places confidence in them, every one wishes them well. This would be the case with us if we were humble; and what happiness we should feel in loving and being loved by all! It seems at first as if this were a question of human respect; but it is inspired by charity, and comes from God and from a desire to resemble Him. Humility is clad in the same garb as charity, which, St. Paul says, "is patient, is kind, envieth not, is not puffed up, is not ambitious" *(1 Corinthians 13:4)*. And it is easy to invest humility with the same virtuous intentions as charity.

MEDITATION 51

*It often happens through our misery that knowledge
hinders the birth of devotion, because knowledge puffeth
up and makes us proud, and pride, which is contrary
to all virtue, is the total ruin of devotion.*

—*St. Francis de Sales*

❧ † ❧

Pride is the root of all our vices, so that, when once we
have uprooted it, those vices will little by little disappear also. This is the true reason of our having to accuse
ourselves of the same sins over and over again in our confessions, because we never confess that pride which is the
root of them all. We do not wonder when we see the fig-
tree bearing its figs year after year, and the apple-tree its
apples. No; because each tree bears its own fruit. In the
same way pride is rooted like a tree in our hearts; and our
sins of anger, envy, hatred, malice and uncharitableness and
rash judgments of others which we confess over and over
again are the fruit of pride; but as we never strike at the
root of this pride these same sins, like clipped branches,
ever sprout out anew. Let us endeavor to eradicate pride
thoroughly, following the advice of St. Bernard: "Put the
axe to the root" and then we shall have great joy and consolation in our own conscience.

King David erred in one thing, for knowing Absalom to be the chief of the rebels he yet commanded that he should neither be killed nor hurt: "Save me the boy Absalom" *(2 Kings, 17:15 [2 Samuel]).* Alas, how many imitators he has found! We know full well that pride is the chief rebel among all our passions, but notwithstanding it is the one which we seem to respect the most, and which we almost fear to offend displaying even a tendency to encourage it.

MEDITATION 52

Far from dazzling me all the titles of nobility appear to me but empty vanity. I have understood those words of the Imitation: "Be not solicitous for the shadow of a great name" (Book 3, 24, 2). I have understood that true greatness is found not in the name but in the soul.

—St. Thérèse of Lisieux

❧ † ❧

Profound humility should exist in every state of life, but exterior acts of humility are not expedient to all. For this reason Holy Writ says: "Beware that thou be not deceived into folly and be humbled" *(Sirach 13:10)*.

We can learn of the pious Esther how to practice humility of heart in the midst of pomp and honors: "Thou knowest my necessity," she cried to God, "that I abominate the sign of my pride" *(Esther 14:16)*. I attire myself in this rich apparel and with these jewels because my position demands it; but You, O Lord, see my heart that through Your grace I am not attached to these things nor to this apparel, and that I only wear them of necessity. Here indeed is a great example of that true inward humility which can be practiced and felt amid external grandeur. But now we. come to the point. This humility of heart must really exist before God, whose eyes behold the most hidden motions of the heart; and if it does not exist what excuse can we allege before the tribunal of God to justify ourselves for not having had it? and the more easily we could have acquired it now, the more inexcusable will it be for us on that day.

MEDITATION 53

Now if the Son was obedient to do His Father's will,
how much more should the servant be obedient
to do his Master's will!

–St. Cyprian of Carthage

The malice of pride lies in reality in the practical contempt which we show for God's will by disobeying it. Thus it is, says St. Augustine, there is pride in every sin committed, "by which we despise the commandments of God." And St. Bernard explains it in this way that God commands us to do His will: "God wishes His will to be done;" and the sinner in his pride prefers his own will to the will of God.

And it is this pride that so greatly augments the grievousness of sin; and how great our sin must be when, knowing in our minds that God deserves to be obeyed by us, we oppose our will to the will of God, whom we know to be worthy of all obedience. What wickedness there is in saying to God, "I will not serve," *(Jeremiah 2:20)* "when we know that all things serve Him" *(Psalm 118[119]:91)*. To give an example of this, let us imagine a person endowed with the noblest qualities possible, such as health, beauty, riches and nobility, and with every natural gift and grace of body and soul. Now, little by little, let us take away from that person all those gifts which come from God. Health and beauty are gifts from God; riches and rank, learning and knowledge, and every other virtue are all from God; body and soul belong to God. And this being so, what remains to this person of his own? Nothing; because all that is more than nothing belongs to God.

MEDITATION 54

There are some who aim at the credit of generosity for pride alone, because they wish thereby to gain the good opinion of the multitude for leaving nothing to themselves; but whilst they are seeking rewards in this life, they are laying up none for the life to come, and having received their reward here they cannot hope for it there.

—St. Ambrose

☙ † ❧

The mistake lies in our having too high an opinion of what the world calls honor, esteem and fame. For however much the world may praise or honor me, it cannot increase my merit or my virtue one jot; and also if the world vituperates me, it cannot take from me anything that I have or that I am in myself. I shall know vanity from truth by the light of that blessed candle which I shall hold in my hand at the hour of my death. What will it profit me then to have been esteemed and honored by the whole world, if my conscience convinces me of sin before God? Ah, what folly it would be for a nobleman, possessing talents which would endear him to his king and make him a favorite at court, if he were to seek rather to be adulated by his servants and vassals, and to find pleasure in such miserable adulation. But it is a far greater folly for a Christian, who might gain the praise and honor of God and of all the angels and saints in heaven, to seek rather to be praised and honored by men and to glory in it. By humility I can please God, the Angels and the Saints; so, is it not a despicable pride that makes me desire the esteem, praise and approbation of men, when we are told that "He is approved whom God commendeth?" *(2 Corinthians 10:18).* The thought of death is profitable in order to acquire humility; and humility helps us greatly to obtain a holy death. St. Catherine of Siena, shortly before her death, was tempted to thoughts of pride and vainglory on account of her own holiness; but to this temptation she answered: "I render thanks to God that in all my life I have never felt any vainglory." Oh, how beautiful to be able to exclaim on one's death-bed: I have never known vainglory.

MEDITATION 55

*I feel that even if there lay upon my conscience all
the crimes one could commit I should lose nothing of
my confidence. Broken-hearted with compunction I would
go and throw myself into the arms of my Savior. I know
that he cherished the Prodigal Son, I have heard His
words to Mary Magdalene, to the adulteress, to the
Samaritan woman.... I know that in one moment all
that multitude of sins would disappear—as a drop
of water cast into a red-hot furnace.*

—St. Thérèse of Lisieux

🌿 † 🌿

It is very easy for a proud person to fall into grave and
terrible sins; and after having fallen to find great dif-
ficulty in accusing himself of them in the Sacrament of
penance; for loving his self-esteem and reputation too
well and fearing to lose them in the eyes of his confessor, he would rather commit a sacrilege than disclose his
weakness. He goes in search of a confessor to whom he is
unknown so as to avoid shame; but since he felt no shame
in sinning, why should he feel so much shame in confessing his sin, if it be not from motives of pride?

It is pride that compels us to withhold our sins in the
confessional and seek to palliate their wickedness with

many excuses. O accursed pride, cause of innumerable sac-
rileges! But O blessed humility! King David was humble
in his repentance, because he did not excuse his sins but
publicly accused himself of them; nor did he lay the blame
of his own sins on others, but attributed them only to his
own wickedness: "I am he that have sinned" *(2 Kings xxiv,
17)*. And the Magdalen also in her repentance did not seek
for Jesus Christ in some hidden spot, but sought Him in
the house of the Pharisee and desired to appear as a sinner
before all the guests. St. Augustine, being truly humble in
his repentance, gave the confession of his sins to the whole
world for his own greater confusion and shame.

MEDITATION 56

We do not deserve any grace from God. Our tendency to sin is always present. The sin of Adam has almost entirely spoiled and soured us, filling us with pride and corrupting every one of us, just as leaven sours, swells and corrupts the dough in which it is placed.

—*St. Louis de Montfort*

❧ † ❧

How the will is moved by grace to co-operate with grace is a mystery which we do not fully comprehend; but it is certain that if we go to heaven we shall then render thanks for our salvation to the mercy of God alone: "The mercies of the Lord will I sing for ever" *(Psalm 88[89]:2)*. We may therefore say with holy King David, and be fully persuaded of its truth, that human nature is weaker and more impotent than we can imagine, because in the nature which we have received of God we have only, through the fall of Adam, ignorance of mind, weakness of reason, corruption of will, disorder of the passions, sickness and misery of the body. We have nothing therefore in which to glory, but in all things we can find fit cause for humiliation. "Humble thyself in all things," *(Sirach 3:20)* says the Holy Ghost, and He does not tell us to humble ourselves in some things only but in all things—in omnibus.

MEDITATION 57

*Believe that others are better than you in the
depths of their souls, although outwardly you
may appear better than they.*

—*St. Augustine of Hippo*

≫ † ≪

Holy humility is inimical to certain subtle speculations;
for instance, you say that you cannot understand how
it is that you are yourself mere nothingness, in doing and
being, because you cannot help knowing that in reality
You are something and can do many things; that you cannot understand why you are the greatest of all sinners,
because you know so many others who are greater sinners
than yourself; nor how it is that you merit all the vituperations of men, when you know that you have done no
actions worthy of blame, but, on the contrary, many worthy of praise.

You should reprove yourself for being still so far from
true humility in thinking that you could grasp the mean-
ing of these things. The truly humble man believes that
he is of himself mere nothingness, a greater sinner than
others, inferior to all, worthy of being reviled by all as
being, more than all others, ungrateful to God. He knows
that this feeling of his conscience is absolutely true, and
does not care to investigate how this comes to be true; his

knowledge is practical, and even if he does not understand himself, and cannot explain to others, with subtle reasoning, what he feels in his heart, he minds as little being unable to explain this as he minds his inability to explain how the eye sees, the tongue speaks, the ear hears. And from this we may infer that it is not necessary to have great talents in order to be humble, and therefore before the tribunal of God it will not be a valid excuse for us to say: "I have not been humble because I did not know, because I did not understand, because I did not study." We can have a good will, a good heart, and yet not be clever; and there is no one who cannot grasp this truth, that from God comes all the good that he possesses and that no one has anything of his own except his own malice. "Destruction is thy own, O Israel: thy help is only in Me," *(Hosea 13:9)* God said by the mouth of His prophet.

MEDITATION 58

*He who with his whole heart draws near unto God
must of necessity be proved by temptation and trial.*

—*St. Albert the Great*

❧ † ❧

Humility is a potent means of subduing temptation,
and in the same way temptations serve to maintain
humility; because it is when we are tempted that we are
practically conscious of our own weakness and the need
we have of Divine grace.

It is for this that God permits us to fall into temptation, reducing us sometimes to the very brink of suc-
cumbing to it, so that we may learn the weakness of our
virtue and how much we need the help of God.

And even in this we can see the infinite wisdom of
God who has so disposed that the demons themselves,
spirits of pride, should contribute to render us humble if
we only knew how to make a good use of our temptations.
Nevertheless, we must remember that in all our temptations the first thing is to exercise that humility which is
derived from a practical knowledge of ourselves and of
how prone we are to evil if God does not stretch out His
hand to restrain us through His grace. Do not let us wait
to learn our weakness till we have fallen; but let us rather
know it beforehand, and the knowledge of it will be an

efficacious means to keep us from falling. "Before sickness take a medicine; humble thyself," *(Sirach 18:20-21)* says Holy Writ. The humble will never want for grace in the time of temptation, and with the help of this grace they will even derive profit from these very temptations; for the merciful providence of God has so disposed it that with the special aid of His grace He will "let no temptation take hold on you" *(1 Corinthians 10:13)*.

MEDITATION 59

How often has He given you His Sacraments?
what inspirations and interior light, what reproofs,
He has given to lead you aright; how often He has
forgiven you, how often delivered you from occasions
of falling; what opportunities He has granted for your
soul's progress! Dwell somewhat on the detail, see
how Loving and Gracious God has been to you.

—St. Francis de Sales

❧ † ❧

We have more opportunities of practicing humility than any other virtue. How many occasions we have of humbling ourselves secretly, in all places, at all times, at every turn—towards God, our fellow-men, and even towards ourselves! With regard to God: how much we have to be ashamed of in our ignorance and ingratitude towards Him; receiving as we do continual benefits of His infinite goodness. Knowing as we do His supreme and infinite Majesty, deserving of all fear; His infinite goodness, worthy of all love; how much we ought to humble ourselves in the thought of how little fear and love we have for Him! With regard to our neighbor: if he be wicked, we may humble ourselves by reflecting that we are capable of becoming suddenly worse than he, and in fact we may consider ourselves worse already if pride predominates within us. If he be good, we must humble ourselves in the thought that he corresponds better than we do to the grace of God and is better than we are by reason of his humility of heart. With regard to ourselves, we need never lack opportunities of humility when we remember our past sins, or consider the faults we commit at present in our daily life, or even when we reflect upon our good works which are all tainted with imperfection, or when we think of the future so filled with tremendous uncertainty: "I know how to be brought low everywhere and in all things," *(Philemon 4:12)* says St. Paul. It is necessary for us to form the good habit of frequently renewing these interior acts of humility. Humility is merely a virtuous habit, but how can we acquire this habit without making repeated acts of humility? Like the habit of humility the habit of pride is acquired through frequent repetition of its acts, and in proportion as the habit of humility is strengthened, the contrary habit of pride becomes weakened and diminished.

MEDITATION 60

Lucifer and his company, which were created in excellent brightness, and were much in the favor of almighty God, they presumptuously offended him in pride, for which they not only lost his favor but also, their marvelous brightness became incontinently horrible, foul, and they were expelled out of the glorious kingdom of heaven that they were in, and thrown into perpetual darkness into the prison of hell.

—St. John Fisher

☙ † ❧

Lucifer sinned once only through pride of thought. Ought we not therefore to consider ourselves worse than Lucifer as our pride has become habitual through the frequent repetition of its acts? We do not consider ourselves proud, because it does not seem to us that we are rash enough in our minds either to believe that we resemble God or to rebel against God; but this is the greatest mistake we can make, because we are full of pride and will not recognize that we are proud. Even if we have not sufficient pride to rebel, to think or to speak against God, we must be fully aware that the pride which prompts our actions is far worse than the pride of thought, and is that pride which is so condemned by St. Paul: "They profess that they know God, but in their works they deny Him" *(Titus 1:16)*. How great is our self-love! Do we ever mortify our passions for the love of God as He Himself has commanded? How often do we prefer to follow our own will instead of the will of God, and as His will is contrary to our own we place ourselves in opposition to Him and desire to gain our own will instead of fulfilling His, valuing the satisfaction of our desires more than the obedience we owe to God! Is not this a worse pride than Lucifer's? for Lucifer only wanted to make himself equal to God, whereas we wish to raise our will above God's. You must humble yourself, O my soul, even below Lucifer, and confess that You are more proud than he!

MEDITATION 61

The only virtue no devil can imitate. If pride made demons out of angels, there is no doubt that humility could make angels out of demons.

—St. John Climacus

❧ † ☙

It is necessary to discern in the Gospel those things which are a counsel and those which are a command. To renounce all that one has and to suffer poverty for the love of God is only a counsel, but to renounce oneself and to be poor of heart is a precept. And in the same way certain exterior humiliations may be only a counsel, but the humility of heart is always a command, and as it is not only possible to fulfill every precept of God's, but also by the help of His grace it becomes easy and sweet to us to practice them; even laymen have many great opportunities of becoming holy simply by the exercise of humility. To make a worldly-minded man a Saint it is sufficient to make him a Christian. When such thoughts as these arise in the secret recesses of the heart: I have made this fortune by my knowledge, by my industry; I have acquired this merit, this reputation by my own worth, my virtue, my ingenuity, it is enough to lift up one's heart to God and say with the Wise Man: "And how could anything endure, if Thou wouldst not?" *(Wisdom 11:26).* O my God, how could I have done the smallest thing, if Thou hadst not willed it?

This is true humility, and in this lies true knowledge and holiness. The soul is holy in measure as it is humble, because in the same measure that it has holiness it has grace, and in the same measure that it has grace it has humility, because grace is only given to the humble.

MEDITATION 62

Oh, what an excellent book is the Passion of Jesus!
There we understand better than in any other book the
malice of sin, and also the mercy and love of God for man.

—St. Alphonsus Liguori

❧ † ❧

What lessons of humility may we not learn from the sacred Passion of our Lord? St. Peter tells us that Jesus Christ suffered for us, leaving us His example so that we might imitate Him: "Christ also suffered for us, leaving you an example that you should follow His steps" *(1 Peter 2:21)*. He does not pretend that we ought to imitate Him by being scourged, crowned with thorns, or nailed to the cross. No; but in all His life, and especially during His Passion, He repeats that important exhortation that we should learn of Him to be humble: "Learn of Me, because I am meek and humble of heart" *(Matthew 11:29)*.

My soul, let us gaze upon the Crucified, "Who endured the cross, despising the shame;" *(Hebrews 12:2)* and by thus confronting His humility with our pride we shall be filled with shame and confusion. And learn yet another lesson. Does it seem well to thee to adore the humility of Jesus crucified and not to wish to imitate Him? To profess to follow Jesus Christ in His religion, which is founded on humility, and yet to feel aversion and even hatred towards this very humility?

MEDITATION 63

Jesus invited us to be like Him, humble of heart.
but what is humility of the heart? It consists in receiving
humiliations from God with a submissive love, in accepting
one's state of life and one's duties whatever they are,
and in not being ashamed of one's condition.

–St. Peter Julian Eymard

❧ † ❧

When we so often hear it said and preached that whoever wishes to be saved must imitate the Saviour,
in what do we imagine that this imitation, which is commanded to us and which is necessary for our salvation,
should consist if not in humility? It is all very well to say
that we must imitate Jesus, but in what must we imitate
Him if not in this humility which is the summing-up of
all the doctrine and examples of His life?

For that Humble One on the Cross will be our Judge;
and His humility will be the standard by which it will be
seen whether we shall be predestined for having imitated
it, or eternally condemned for having rejected it. It is necessary for us to be firmly convinced of this truth. God does
not propose that we should all imitate His Incarnate Son
in all the mysteries of His life. The solitude and austerity
which He endured in the desert are reserved only for the
imitation of anchorites. In His teaching He is only to be

imitated by the apostles and preachers of His Gospel. In the working of miracles only those can imitate Him who have been chosen by Him to be co-adjutors in the establishment of the Faith. In the sufferings and agony of Calvary none may imitate Him but those to whom He has given the privilege of Martyrdom.

But that humility of heart practiced by Jesus Christ in every hour of His life on earth is given to all of us as an example which we are compelled to follow, and to this imitation God has united our eternal salvation: "Unless you be converted and become as a little child" *(Matthew xviii, 3)*.

MEDITATION 64

The Blessed Virgin had always the majesty of God,
and her own nothingness, present to her mind.

—*St. Bernadine of Siena*

✾ † ✾

After Jesus Christ, Who is King of the humble, what a beautiful example of humility we have in the Blessed Virgin Mary who is their Queen! No creature ever surpassed her in merit, or exceeded her in humility. By her humility she deserved to be the Mother of God, and by humility only she maintained the dignity and honor of the sublime Maternity.

Let us picture Mary in her room at Nazareth when it was announced to her by the Archangel Gabriel that the time had come for the Eternal Word to take flesh in her womb, through the operation of the Holy Ghost. She showed no sign of pride at being blest among women and chosen for such a high honor, but on the contrary she was distressed and "was troubled at his saying," *(Luke 1:29)* without being able to understand why she was chosen for so great an honor. And what does she exclaim? I,—the Mother of God! I, a vile creature, to become the Mother of God! I am but His servant, and it would be too much honor for me even to be His handmaid. "Behold the handmaid of the Lord" *(Luke 1:38)*. Thus Mary humbled herself as much as lay in her power; and she continued in this deep humility all through her life, behaving in all things as the servant of the Lord, without ever attributing to herself the slightest glory for being His Mother. What a beautiful example for us! Therefore, if we have devotion to our Lady we ought to try and imitate her in her humility; and in all the prayers, Communions and mortifications that we offer in her honor let us always ask her to obtain for us through her intercession the grace of holy humility. There is no grace that our Blessed Lady asks so willingly of Jesus for her devotees, and which Jesus concedes so willingly to Mary as the grace of humility, since both Jesus and Mary hold this virtue in singular affection.

MEDITATION 65

And therefore in beginning the Divine Law He begins
with humility, and sets before us a great reward, saying,
"And ye shall find rest for your souls." This is the highest
reward, you shall not only be made useful to others, but
shall make yourself to have peace; and He gives you the
promise of it before it comes, but when it is come, you shall
rejoice in perpetual rest. And that they might not be afraid
because He had spoken of a burden, therefore, He adds,
"For my yoke is pleasant, and my burden light."

—St. John Chrysostom

࿔ ☨ ࿔

O my soul, it is through humility that we shall reach
Paradise. And what shall we do in paradise? There the
practice of all other virtues ceases and only charity and
humility remain. We shall see God, and in seeing Him we
shall know that He is the infinite Good; and this perfect
knowledge will bring with it more perfect love, and the
more we love God, the better we shall know Him, and
the better we know Him, the more humble we shall be,
practicing humility through all eternity like the ancients
seen in the Apocalypse by the Apostle St. John: "Who
fell on their faces and adored God, saying, We give Thee
thanks, O Lord God almighty, who art, and who wast, and

who art to come" *(Apocrypha 11:17).* Let us begin to practice on earth those virtues which we hope to practice for ever and ever through all ages in Heaven: "Our Lord Jesus Christ humbled Himself, becoming obedient unto death, even to the death of the cross. For which cause God also hath exalted Him, and hath given Him a name which is above all names" *(Philippians 2:8-9).* "Deliver me, O Lord, from the evil man, rescue me from the unjust man" *(Psalm 139:2).* Who is this wicked and unjust man from whom I pray to be delivered? He is my inner self who is all vice, corruption and pride, and it is the same as if I were to say: "Deliver me, O Lord, from myself, that is, give me grace to amend and reform myself in order that I may no longer be that earthly, worldly and proud creature which I have been hitherto, dominated by passion, but that I may be renewed, and may conform to the spirit of my humble Lord and Master Jesus Christ." "Deliver me, O Lord, from the evil man; rescue me from the unjust man."

MEDITATION 66

*Do not imitate those who deceive themselves by saying:
"I will sin and then go to confession." How do you know
that you will have time to make your confession? Is it not
madness to wound oneself, in the hope that a doctor
will be found who will heal the wound?*

—St. John Bosco

The more essential the grace we are asking of God is for
us, the more necessary is humility. Before going however to the tribunal of penance do you humble yourself,
and ask God to give you that sorrow for your sins which
is necessary for the validity of the Sacrament? As this sorrow must be supernatural, it is certain that you could never
attain to it of yourself, however much you were to try and
force yourself to feel it. God alone can give it to you, and
it is equally certain that this is not a debt which He owes
you, but a great grace which it pleases Him to confer upon
you out of His goodness alone and without any merit on
your part. If, however, you desire to receive this grace, you
must ask it with humility, protesting from your heart that
you do not deserve it, that you are unworthy to receive it,
and that you only hope for it through the merits of Jesus

Christ. But do you practice this humility, which is, one may say, of precept for you, because it is an essential means of obtaining contrition?

MEDITATION 67

*Dear Lord, you know my weakness. Each morning
I resolve to be humble, and in the evening I recognize
that I have often been guilty of pride.*

—St. Thérèse of Lisieux

❧ † ❧

Your resolutions must be constant and efficacious, but
cannot be so without the special help of God. Do
you ever think of humbling yourself and asking for that
help, knowing and confessing your instability and weakness, and that you are not capable of yourself to keep the
smallest resolution, either from morning till night or even
from one hour to another?

It is for this reason that you so often fall over and
over again into the same faults, because you are lacking
in humility. The truly humble man is altogether diffident
about himself, and putting all his trust in God, is helped in
the most admirable way by Him. "Humble thyself to God
and wait for His hands" *(Sirach 13:9).*

How many times do you not say: "I have taken this
firm resolution, and I mean to keep it, I am not afraid
of breaking it," trusting iniquitously in yourself, without
acknowledging the Divine help in any way? Take care that
you may not be counted among those reprobates "who

were destroyed trusting to their own strength" *(Sirach 16:8)*. If you even presume only a little upon yourself, that little can be the cause of great ruin, according to the prediction of Job: "They are lifted up for a little while, and shall not stand, and shall be brought down" *(Job 24:4)*.

MEDITATION 68

*The more subtly vain confession is, the more dangerously
hurtful it is, as when, for instance, we are not ashamed
to reveal our shameful deeds, not because we are humble
but that we may seem to be so. What more perverse or
shameful than that confession, the guardian of humility,
should take service under the banner of pride?*

—*St. Bernard of Clairvaux*

There are some people who, under the pretext of making acts of humility, desire from time to time to accuse
themselves in their confession of some grave and shameful
sin of their past life. If peradventure you are among these,
beware lest this arise more from a desire to appear humble than to be humble in reality. Self-love is cunning, and
knows how to work secretly.

This kind of humility is not always desirable even outside the confessional, because it can easily lead us to create
scandal by speaking of certain sins which should not even
be named. If you have this strange fault, there is no reason
why you should pride yourself on it, but you should rather
be ashamed of it; for, as the holy abbot says: "What species
of pride can this be, that thou wouldst fain be better by
what thou appearest to be worse? That thou canst not be
thought holy without seeming to be wicked?"

MEDITATION 69

Humility was extolled by Christ; and surely in this Sacrament (of the Eucharist) He preaches an unrivalled humility, which disdains no dwelling, but consents to come like a guest to any heart, even one that is defiled.

—St. Thomas Aquinas

❧ † ☙

How necessary humility is, in order that you should approach Holy Communion worthily, your own faith can teach you. But in your preparation for that Divine Sacrament and in your thanksgiving, do you make due acts of humility? It is true that you kneel down in all exterior humility and beat your breast at the "Domine non sum dignus," but have you really that true humility of heart which is becoming to such a holy function?

The centurion was sanctified when he received Jesus Christ in his own house, because he prepared himself to receive Him with deep humility and said, more from his heart than with his lips, "Lord, I am not worthy that Thou shouldst enter under my roof" *(Matthew 8:8)*. This mystery more than others calls for humility, and when the Son of God took flesh in the womb of the Blessed Virgin Mary, it was specially by virtue of her humility, "because He hath regarded the humility of His handmaid" *(Luke 1:48)*. Oh, if you were to reflect that it is a God you are going to receive; but do you think of this as God Himself exhorts you to do? "Be still and see that I am God" *(Psalm 45[46]:11).*

MEDITATION 70

There is more value in a little study of humility and in a single act of it than in all the knowledge in the world.

—St. Teresa of Ávila

❧ † ❧

How do you humble your intellect in regard to the mysteries of the Catholic Faith? Are you curious in seeking and wishing to know the reasons for those things which the Church proposes for your belief, inclining to surrender yourself more to human reasoning than to Divine authority? In matters of faith it is most necessary to practice humility, and the more humble our belief, the more honor it gives to God.

It is for this reason that Holy Writ, after having said that God is honored by the humble, exhorts us emphatically to humble our intellect: "He is honored by the humble. Seek not the things that are too high for thee, and search not into things which are above thy ability; but the things that God hath commanded thee, think on them always, and in many of his works be not curious" *(Sirach 3:22)*. When it is a question of faith, the Apostle teaches us that we must not seek to know the why and wherefore, but to humble any height of our understanding in lowly reverence to Jesus Christ, "bringing into captivity every understanding unto the obedience of God" *(2 Corinthians 10:5)*. This is most necessary.

And especially when we have temptations against faith, it is necessary that we should humble ourselves immediately, without entering into argument or dispute with the devil. But are you prudent in taking these measures at once, and do you say with King David, I will not pause to consider these speculations in "great matters nor in things too wonderful for me?" *(Psalm 130[131]:2)*.

MEDITATION 71

*That man is truly humble who converts
humiliation into humility.*

—*St. Bernard of Clarivaux*

❧ † ❧

The best means to oblige God to deliver us from our troubles is to humble ourselves, and King David testifies to this by his own experience in *Psalm 114[115]:4, 6,* "I met with trouble and sorrow, I was humbled and He delivered me." Do you ever practice this means of humbling yourself in your troubles, protesting that you have merited them, and deserve them if for no other reason than on account of your pride?

God sends adversity to you to humble you, and He humbles you so that from this humiliation you may learn humility. But what fruit of humility have you gathered from all the adversity you have had hitherto? Can you say, as Moses said to the Hebrews: "We have rejoiced for the days in which Thou hast humbled us?" *(Psalm 89[90]:15).*

MEDITATION 72

If weak and imperfect souls like mine felt what I feel,
none would despair of reaching the summit of the
Mountain of Love, since Jesus does not ask for great
deeds, but only for gratitude and self-surrender.

—St. Thérèse of Lisieux

☙ ✝ ☞

If you have any good quality, either bodily or spiritual, and if you have done any good work, do you recognize that it all comes from, God, attributing all the glory to God as due to Him alone? "To the only God be honour and glory" *(2 Timothy 1:17)*. In this, says St. Paul, we discern the spirit of God which is the spirit of humility, from the spirit of the world which is the spirit of pride, because whoever has the spirit of God acknowledges that all that he has is simply a gift from God. "Now we have received not the spirit of the world but the spirit that is of God, that we may know the things that are given us from God" *(1 Corinthians 1:12)*.

But of what use would this recognition that everything comes from God be, except to refer all things to Him and to thank Him? Do you thank God for the many blessings which you are constantly receiving from Him— from your very heart, with true humility, believing yourself to be so miserable that you would fall into every sin, and even into Hell itself, if God did not come to your help? "Unless the Lord had been my helper, my soul had almost dwelt in Hell" *(Psalm 93:17)*.

MEDITATION 73

*I will humble myself more for those virtues which
I lack than pride myself on those I possess.*

—St. Augustine of Hippo

❧ † ❧

Examine those virtues which you imagine that you possess. Have you prudence, temperance, fortitude, justice, modesty, humility, chastity, humbleness of spirit, charity, obedience, and many other virtues that may be necessary or suitable to your condition? If you have a few of these, in what degree do you possess them?

But I will say more: and that is, examine yourself first, and see whether you really have this virtue that you think you possess. What I mean to say is: is it a real virtue, or perhaps only a disposition of your natural temperament, be it melancholy, sanguine or phlegmatic? And even should this virtue be real, is it a Christian virtue or purely a human one? Every act of virtue which does not proceed from a supernatural motive, in order to bring us to everlasting bliss, is of no value. And in the practice of virtue, do you join to your external actions the inward and spiritual acts of the heart? O true Christian virtues, I fear that in me you are nothing but beautiful outward appearances! I deserve the reproach of God's word: "Because thou sayest:

I am rich, and made wealthy, and have need of nothing; and knowest not that thou art wretched and miserable, and poor and blind and naked" *(Apocrypha 3:17).*

MEDITATION 74

The humble man enjoys peace in the midst of many vexations, because his trust is in God, not in the world. Hence, you must not think that you have made any progress until you look upon yourself as inferior to all others.

—Thomas à Kempis

❧ † ❧

How do you behave to your inferiors? It is towards these that you must exercise humility most of all. "The greater thou art," says the inspired word, "the more humble thyself in all things" *(Sirach 3:20)*. And although they are inferior as regards their condition of life, remember always that before God they are your equals. "Knowing that the Lord both of them and yourself is in Heaven, and there is no respect of persons with Him" *(Ephesians 6:9)*.

In this way you will become kind and considerate, as St. Paul advises when He says: "Consenting to be humble" *(Romans 12:16)*. Do you command them haughtily and imperiously, against the express wish of God Who does not desire you to behave to your inferiors "as lording it?" *(1 Peter 5:3)*. And when you are obliged to correct them, do you do it in the proper spirit: "In the spirit of meekness," as the Apostle teaches us, "considering thyself lest thou also be tempted?" *(Galatians vi, 1)*.

MEDITATION 75

We are very apt to speak of ourselves as nothing,
as weakness itself, as the off-scouring of the earth; but
we should be very much vexed to be taken at our word
and generally considered what we call ourselves. On the
contrary we pretend to take the lowest place, with the full
intention of being honorably called to come up higher.
But true humility does not affect to be humble, and is not
given to make a display in lowly words. It seeks not only
to conceal other virtues, but above all it seeks and desires
to conceal itself; and if it were lawful to tell lies, or feign or
give scandal, humility would perhaps sometimes affect
a cloak of pride in order to hide itself utterly.

—St. Francis de Sales

❧ † ☙

There is also another kind of humility which is false, and against which we are warned by the Holy Spirit when He says: "Be not lowly in thy wisdom, lest being humbled thou be deceived into folly" *(Sirach 13:11)*. If you possess the talent of teaching, counselling, helping and doing good to the souls of others, and you then retire, saying, as if from humility: "I am not good enough;" or if you are in a position when it is your duty to correct, punish or exercise authority, and you abandon it from motives of humility, this is not true humility but weakness and cowardice, and as far as externals are concerned we must observe the rule of the holy father St. Augustine: "Lest whilst humility is unduly observed the authority of the ruler be undermined amongst those who ought to be submissive."

Much as I should praise you for regarding yourself as inferior in merit to all those below you, "in the knowledge of your heart," as St. Gregory says so well; yet it must not be to the detriment of your office, lessening its superiority. For being in a superior position does not prevent you from being humble of heart; but this humility must not be an impediment to the exercise of your authority.

MEDITATION 76

In truth, the soul can possess no better insight for knowledge than to perceive its own nothingness.

—*St. Angela of Foligno*

The humility of affection consists in the recognition that we are more miserable than any one else, and to love to be regarded as such by others. To be vile and abject in our own eyes through the knowledge that we have of ourselves is the humility of necessity, to which we are compelled by the obvious truth of it; but to have a sincere desire to be looked upon as vile and abject by others, this is true and virtuous humility of the heart. Take heed lest, while you do not esteem yourself, you should still wish to be esteemed by others. This would be to love something that does not exist, to love a lie.

How far you are from that humility of affection! How you fear lest any of your faults should be revealed, and how many excuses and justifications you make, in order that this imputation of a fault which you have really committed may not diminish the esteem in which others hold you. In order to be more esteemed, you try to show your ability and talent, and if you have but little ability and little talent, how often you pretend you have more in the hope of being esteemed still more!

MEDITATION 77

If you suffer a false accusation, defend yourself quietly, denying the fact; this is but due respect for truth and your neighbor's edification. But if after you have made your true and legitimate defense you are still accused, do not be troubled, and do not try to press your defense—you have had due respect for truth, have the same now for humility.

—St. Francis de Sales

☙ ✝ ☙

It is this humility of affection, this humility of the heart taught us by Jesus Christ, which makes us as little children, and enables us to enter into the kingdom of Heaven. But what shame for you if, when you examine yourself, you find you have not even the shadow of such humility! If you happen to hear that others have spoken uncharitably of you, and maligned you, are you not perturbed, disquieted, grieved, displeased, distressed? How you resent it when you think some one has wronged you or not treated you with proper respect! Are you suspicious, easily offended, and punctilious about all things that concern your honor and dignity? I am not speaking now of that honor which is founded on virtue, but of that despicable honor which depends on the opinion of the world. What value do you set upon this honor? Do you take offence easily, considering yourself injured by every little adverse word, every slight that you receive from others, becoming angry and irritated, nourishing aversion and rancor, demanding humble apologies and satisfaction, and showing yourself unforgiving, irreconcilable towards them: fearing to lose your dignity, if you consented to make peace like a good Christian? If such be the case, where is your humility, either of knowledge or affection, which is necessary for your salvation?

MEDITATION 78

If you wish to go to extremes, let it be in sweetness, patience, humility and charity.

—St. Philip Neri

❧ † ❧

If the humble man becomes aware that he has offended or injured his neighbor, he immediately humbles himself, apologizes and asks to be forgiven, manifesting sorrow for the offense he has given. The humble man always fears to be dictatorial when carried away by his zeal, and therefore proceeds with much circumspection, exercising his zeal more on himself than on others. He gives his opinion modestly, and submits it to that of others without obstinacy. But you?

The humble man respects and reverences those above him, and he is kind and courteous to the poorest of the poor; and in this he only follows the teaching of the Preacher: "Make thyself affable to the congregation of the poor, and humble thy soul to the ancient" *(Sirach 4:7)*. Is this the way in which you generally behave? The humble man does not seek to appear humble by affectation of manner; on the contrary, if he knows that others believe him to be humble, he feels a painful confusion. His nature is to be sincere, simple and straightforward. He is of lowly bearing, and lowly too has he kept his human caprices and his pride. He is not hard and haughty, but gentle, reverent and obedient.

MEDITATION 79

It is easier for the proud man to see within themselves that which is pleasing to them, than that which is displeasing.

—St. Gregory the Great

⚜ ✝ ⚜

Do you forget your own nothingness? Have you any self-esteem? If such be the case you are a seducer, a deceiver of your own self, because, as St. Paul says: Whoever believes himself to be something "deceiveth himself" *(Galatians 6:3)*. Do you delight and glory in your knowledge, your power, your riches, or in some other gift natural or moral? Remember the word God spoke by the Prophet Jeremiah: "Let not the wise man glory in his wisdom, and let not the strong man glory in his strength, and let not the rich man glory in his riches" *(Jeremiah 1:23)*. And again by St. Paul: "We ought not to please ourselves" *(Romans 15:1)*.

This delight and glory insinuates itself insensibly, but he who is humble notices it quickly and repels it as being nothing but vanity and only puffing up and filling the heart with pride.

The proud man dwells more willingly on the little good he does, on the little devotion he feels, than on the thought of the evil he has committed and which he does daily. He puts behind him the multitude of his sins, so that he need not be ashamed and humble himself;

and he reflects often upon certain of his minute exercises of Christian piety, so as to indulge his self-complacency. Perhaps you also have this tendency.

MEDITATION 80

However great the work that God may achieve by an individual, he must not indulge in self-satisfaction. He ought rather to be all the more humbled, seeing himself merely as a tool which God has made use of.

−St. Vincent de Paul

☙ † ☙

Humility teaches us also to hold ourselves unworthy of any good that we may possess, even to the very air that we breathe, and to hold ourselves worthy of all the evils and vituperations of the world. Such are the thoughts of the humble man. He always keeps before his eyes the sins he has committed, and his malicious tendency to commit them again. Therefore he esteems himself worse than the infidels who have not the light of grace, while he has also that of faith; worse than all sinners, that do not realize the gravity of sin, and who have not received so much help of grace as he has; worse than the Jews, "For if they had known it, they would never have crucified the Lord of glory" *(1 Corinthians 2:8)*; worse even than the demons, who sinned only once in thought, whilst he has sinned so often even in action. But do you ever stop to consider these things seriously?

MEDITATION 81

*Nothing in man is further removed from humility
than reliance upon his own virtue.*

−St. Gregory the Great

❧ † ☙

Do you place yourself in dangerous occasions, saying:
"I will not fall into sin," thus presuming too much
on your own strength? Are you disturbed and agitated at
the thought of the faults you commit, and of your slow
progress in acquiring virtue? This is pride, and comes from
your presumption in thinking you can do great things of
your own strength. But it is necessary to humble ourselves and yet not be discouraged; I shall be more humble, if I reflect upon those virtues which I ought to have,
and have not.

Are you prudent, not trusting in your own ingenuity
nor in your own opinions, without caring to ask advice,
especially in matters of great importance? This is a great
sin against humility, and the Holy Spirit thus admonishes
you: "Lean not on thy own prudence: be not wise in thy
own conceit" *(Proverbs 3:5-7)*. And St. Jerome calls that
pride intolerable by which we give others to understand
that we are so wise we do not need their advice: "Pride is
unbearable, but to account oneself nothing needs counsel."

MEDITATION 82

Another species of evil words consists in flattery,
which is willingly heard by men; and yet it produces
pride and vanity, the former of which is the queen
of vices, and is most hateful to God.

—St. Robert Bellarmine

❧ † ❧

When you hear yourself praised, what precautions do you take? Self-love is quick to mingle some grain of its own incense with that which it receives from others. I mean by this that through the corruption of our nature we are very ready to approve these praises as if they were truly and justly due to us, and to flatter ourselves with vainglory; but all this comes from want of humility. St. Augustine, speaking of this pleasure which we derive from being praised, addresses this prayer to God: "Lord, put this folly far from me," for he held it as a real madness to take pleasure in vanity and deceits.; and when he heard others praise him, he pondered upon the knowledge he had of himself and upon the justice of God, saying in his own heart: "I know myself better than they know me, but God knows me better than I know myself."

A heart that is truly humble, says St. Gregory, always fears to hear its own praises, because it fears that this praise may either be false or may rob it of the merit and reward promised to true virtue. "If the heart is truly humble, the good that it hears of itself it either fails to recognize or fears lest the hope of future title to reward be changed for some passing favor."

MEDITATION 83

To a humble soul nothing is more wonderful than to hear its own excellence; thus, to Mary's saying, "How shall this be?" the Angel brings forward a proof, not to take away her belief but rather to dispel her wonder.

—St. Thomas Aquinas

༝ ✝ ༝

The humble man, says St. Thomas, is amazed when anyone speaks well of him, and there is nothing that astonishes him more than to hear himself praised. Thus the Blessed Virgin, when she heard from the Archangel Gabriel that she was to become the Mother of God, had such a lowly opinion of herself that she marveled greatly that she should be exalted to such an eminent dignity.

But pride may even insinuate itself into this very contempt of praise, as St. Augustine says: "A man is often foolishly proud of his own foolish contempt of himself."

But if it be necessary for us to praise those who are present, it is not less necessary to exercise discretion and prudence in so doing, as St. Augustine also teaches: "Lest the most dangerous temptation be found in the love of giving praise." Adulation is always pernicious, whether we adulate ourselves or others.

MEDITATION 84

The man who follows his own will independently
of God's, is guilty of a kind of idolatry. Instead
of adoring God's will, he, in a certain sense, adores
his own. The greatest glory we can give to God is to
do his will in everything. Our Redeemer came on
earth to glorify his heavenly Father and to teach
us by his example how to do the same.

−*St. Alphonsus Liguori*

✠

Pride holds the first place among the deadly sins, and St. Thomas not only places it amongst the deadly sins, but above them, as transcending them all, the king of vices which includes in his cortège all the other vices, therefore it is called in Holy Scripture: "The root of all evil," *(Timothy 6:10)* "The beginning of all sin" *(Sirach 10:15)*. because as the root of the tree is hidden under the earth and sends all its strength up into the branches, so pride remains hidden in the heart and secretly influences every sin through its action. Thus, whenever we commit a mortal sin, we are in reality opposing and directing our own will against the will of God.

Job speaks thus of the sinner: "He hath strengthened himself against the Almighty," *(Job 15:25)* and in this sense one can also say of pride that it is the greatest of all sins, because the proud rebel against God, setting themselves in opposition to God, nor do they mind displeasing God in order to please themselves, as St. Augustine says: "Abandoning God, he seeks his own will, and by so doing draws near to nothingness, hence the proud according to Scripture are called doers of their own will," which is to say with St. Paul: "Lovers of themselves." And the same holy father makes this reflection, that even venial sins committed more from frailty than from malice may become mortal if they are aggravated by pride.

MEDITATION 85

*For the vice of pride is a near neighbor to good deeds,
and arrogance ever lies in wait hard by virtue: because
it is hard for him that lives praise-worthily not to
be caught by man's praise unless, as it is written,
"he that boasts, let him boast in the Lord."*

—St. Leo the Great

☙ † ❧

Let us now consider wherein lies the terrible danger of
this vice of pride.

(1) Because while all other vices destroy only their
opposite virtues, as wantonness destroys chastity, greedi-
ness temperance, and anger gentleness, etc., pride destroys
all virtue, and is according to St. Gregory like a cancer
which not only eats away one limb but attacks the whole
body: "Like a widespread pestilential disease."

(2) Because the other vices are to be feared only when
we are disposed to evil; but pride, says St. Augustine, insinuates itself even when we are trying to do good. "Other
vices are to be feared in sins, pride is to be feared even in
good deeds." And Saint Isidore says: "Pride is worse than
every other vice from the fact that it springs even from
virtue and its guilt is less felt."

(3) Because after having fought against and overcome
the other vices we may justly rejoice, but as soon as we

begin to rejoice that we have triumphed over pride it triumphs over us, and becomes victorious over us in that very act for which we are praising ourselves for conquering it. St. Augustine says: "When a man rejoices that he has overcome pride, he lifts up his head for very joy and says: Behold, I triumph thus because you triumphed."

(4) Because if the other vices are of quick growth, we can also rid ourselves of them quickly; but pride is the first vice we learn, and it is also the last to leave us as St. Augustine says "For those who are returning to God, pride is the last thing to be overcome, as it was the first cause of their leaving God."

(5) Because as we have need of some special grace of God in order to enable us to do any of those good works that pertain to our eternal salvation, so there is no vice which prevents the influx of grace so much as pride; because "God resists the proud" *(James 4:6)*.

(6) Because pride is the characteristic and most significant sign of the reprobate, as St. Gregory says: "Pride is the most manifest sign of the lost."

(7) Because the other vices are easily recognizable, and therefore it is easy to hate them and to amend; but pride is a vice that is not so easily known because it goes masked and disguised in many forms, even putting on the semblance of virtue and the very appearance of humility; thus being a hidden vice it is less easy to escape from it, as is taught in the maxim of St. Ambrose: "Hidden things are more difficult to avoid than things known."

MEDITATION 86

*But the perverted will struggles towards the ultimate
good by devious ways, yearning after satisfaction, yet led
astray by vanity and deceived by wickedness. Ah, if you
wish to attain to the consummation of all desire, so that
nothing unfulfilled will be left, why weary yourself
with fruitless efforts, running hither and thither,
only to die long before the goal is reached?*

—*St. Bernard of Clarivaux*

꒳ † ꒳

This last danger is for us the greatest of all, and all the
more because we ourselves seem to co-operate so as
not to recognize this vice, inventing titles, colors, artifices
to conceal its ugliness, and studying innumerable pretexts
in order to deceive ourselves into believing that pride is
not pride, and does not reign in our heart at the very
moment when it is more dominant than ever.

As humility is generally called weak and contemptible
by the blind lovers of this world, so pride is called courage
and greatness, and the proud are said to be spirited, dig-
nified, of noble behavior and good judgment, sustaining
their position with honor, maintaining their reputation,
keeping up their rank and fulfilling the duties of their state.
What a vocabulary of vanity! But let us set against it the

vocabulary of truth which was used by Job: "I have said to rottenness, Thou art my father; to worms, my mother and my sister" *(Job 17:4).*

MEDITATION 87

*When the proud delight in their own excellence
they recede from the excellence of truth.*

—St. Augustine of Hippo

❧ † ❧

This alone I ask of you, that if you have unfortunately
been deceived by others, you will at least not deceive
yourselves. Study to know your own ills, if you wish to
be cured of them. I recommend you only to apply yourselves to learn the truth and profit by this advice, that if
the knowledge of this truth seems difficult to you, it is a
sign that you are proud.

It is St. Thomas himself who will convince you of this.
You can learn truth in two ways, that is by the intellect
and by the affections. The proud man does not know it
by his intellect, because God hides it from him, as Christ
said: "Thou hast hid these things from the wise and prudent;" *(Matthew 11:25)* and still less will he know it with
his affection, because no one who takes pleasure in vanity
can take pleasure in truth.

The proud man does not take any pleasure in sermons,
meditations, instructions concerning eternal truth, in fact
they are wearisome to him. If you discover any signs of this
in yourself, you must at once conclude that you are proud,
and humble yourself a little, O you who read this doctrine,

in order that the eternal Father of all light may give you light even as Christ said: "I confess to Thee, O Father, Who hast revealed them to little ones" *(Matthew 11:25).*

MEDITATION 88

*Would it not be the extreme of folly in a brute animal
(were it gifted with reason) to glory in the gilded trappings
of which it knows it may be stripped at the beck of
its master? The proud man is blind.*

—St. Alphonsus Liguori

❧ † ❧

A nother way in which we can sin in our actions by
pride is when, knowing and admitting that we have
received such and such a gift of God, we nevertheless attribute it inwardly to our own merit and desire that others
should do so likewise, and in our exterior demeanor we
behave as if we had indeed deserved to receive these gifts.
It was thus that Lucifer sinned through pride; for being
infatuated with his own beauty and nobility, and although
he recognized that God was the author of it all, he nevertheless had the presumption to think that he had merited
it himself and was worthy to sit beside God in the highest
Heaven, "I will ascend into Heaven" *(Isaiah 14:13)*.

And, therefore, St. Bernard reproves him, saying: "O
proud soul, what work hast thou done that thou shouldst
take thy rest?" What hast thou done, O bold one, to
deserve such an honor? And it is thus that those reprobates sinned through pride to whom allusion is made in
Luke 17:9, who, like the Pharisee, gave thanks to God for

the good they did and the evil they left undone: "O God, I give Thee thanks," etc.; but yet, at the same time, they had the presumption to consider themselves of singular merit, "trusting in themselves."

MEDITATION 89

When a man sees that whatever good he has
is from the mercy of God and not from his own merits,
he ceases to be proud.

—*St. Augustine of Hippo*

※ † ※

All those who sin by presuming that they have deserved any good whatsoever of God are convicted of pride, because by attesting to their own merit they make God a debtor of this grace, which would no longer be grace if we had deserved it. We may well be permitted, with Job, to say that by our sins we have deserved God's anger and every kind of evil: "Oh, that my sins, whereby I have deserved wrath, were weighed in a balance" *(Job 6:2)* but we cannot say that we deserve grace or any good, as St. Paul says: "If by grace it is not now by works, otherwise grace is no more grace."

And each one of us should say with the same humble St. Paul, "By the grace of God I am what I am" *(1 Corinthians 15:10)*. If I am rich, noble, sane, or possess any other gifts, it all comes from God who has made me thus, not because of my own merits, but solely through His Own mercy and goodness. Whether I abstain from evil or whether I do good, I owe it all not to my own merit, but to the grace of God Who assists me with His mercy; "By the grace of God I am what I am." And anyone who ascribes what he is or what he has to his own merits, is guilty of pride, and appropriates to himself what he ought to give to the mercy and grace of God. In this way, holy Church wisely ends her prayers with these words: "Through Jesus Christ our Lord," etc. And by this we protest to the Divine Majesty that we ask the gifts mentioned in those prayers through the merits of Jesus Christ, and that, if our prayers are heard, it will only be through the merits of Jesus Christ.

This is a point which is worthy of all attention so that we may not fall through inadvertence into most terrible pride. And St. Augustine urges us to remember that not only all the good we have comes from God, but also that we have it only through His mercy and not through our own merits.

MEDITATION 90

The gate of Heaven is very low;
only the humble can enter it.

—*Blessed Elizabeth Seton*

꧁ † ꧂

We can sin through pride when we attribute to ourselves some good—of any kind whatsoever—which we do not really possess, but whether it be that we esteem ourselves for that imaginary good which exists only in our thoughts, and desire others to esteem us for it also, or whether we really possess it, or whether again we only desire to have this good which we have not in order to be able to boast of it and glory in it, all this is detestable pride.

It was in this way that the Bishop of Laodicea sinned by esteeming himself rich in merit when he was merely contemptible; and therefore God told him that he would vomit him out of His mouth. "I will begin to vomit thee out of My mouth, because thou sayest, I am rich and have need of nothing, and knowest not that thou art miserable and poor" *(Apocrypha iii, 16, 17)*. And it is with this kind of pride that all sin who either esteem themselves or who seek to be esteemed by others in word or deed for more riches, knowledge, rank or virtue than they really have.

It may be an act of virtue to desire these things for some honorable end, for instance to desire more knowledge in order to be able to serve holy Church, to desire riches in order to be able to give more alms; but to desire these things in order not to seem inferior to others or to acquire more esteem, is only pride, and oh, how few there are who are not infected with this pride! One for one thing, and one for another, almost all men seek to be esteemed above what they really are—and this without the slightest scruple.

MEDITATION 91

*In like manner it is possible to be honorably elated
when your thoughts indeed are not lowly, but your mind
by greatness of soul is lifted up towards virtue. This
loftiness of mind is seen in a cheerfulness amidst sorrow;
or a kind of noble dauntlessness in trouble; a contempt
of earthly things, and a conversation in heaven. And
this loftiness of mind seems to differ from that elevation
which is engendered of pride, just as the stoutness of
a well-regulated body differs from the swelling
of the flesh which proceeds from dropsy.*

–St. Basil

༺ † ༻

We sin through pride when we use any gift we may
possess in order to appear distinguished or to think
ourselves better than others, and to be more esteemed and
honored than they. Whatever good we have, whether of
body or soul, of nature, fortune or grace, is a gift of God,
and to use these gifts in order to try and be more conspicuous than others is pride.

It is with this pride that the Pharisee in the Temple
regarded his own goodness, and placed himself above others, especially the publican. "I am not as the rest of men,
extortioners, unjust, adulterers, as also is this publican"

(Luke 18:11). He esteemed himself above all, and was in reality the proudest of all. It was with this pride, too, that the disciples sinned when they glorified in their singular gift of being able to cast out devils: "And they returned with joy, saying: 'Lord, the devils also are subject to us,'" *(Luke 10:17)* and our blessed Lord answered them most justly: "I saw Satan like lightning falling from Heaven," as if He almost meant to say "Take care that you do not exalt yourself like the proud Lucifer, lest you fall as he did."

Whoever wishes to exalt himself above others imitates Lucifer who desired to be first among the Angels and nearest to the throne of God. This was the sin of Lucifer when he dwelt upon his desire to be exalted: "And thou saidest in thy heart, I will ascend" *(Isaiah 14:13)*. And those who are always scheming for their own advancement, and are discontented with their own state sin even as Lucifer sinned: "I will ascend;" and we ought to guard against this diabolical sin, as St. Paul says: "Lest being puffed up with pride we fall into the judgment of the devil" *(1 Timothy 3:6)*.

MEDITATION 92

*If I were unfaithful, if I committed the slightest infidelity
springing from pride, say, if I said "I have acquired this
or that virtue," fearful troubles would follow, and I
could no longer accept death with resignation.*

—St. Thérèse of Lisieux

🌿 † 🌿

The holy pope St. Gregory discerns pride in all kinds of
people and describes its characteristics. Some, he says,
are proud of their possessions, others of their eloquence,
some are proud of mundane things and some of things
of the Church and the gifts of God, although blinded by
vanity we are unable to discern it; and whether we exalt
ourselves above others on account of worldly glory, or
of spiritual gifts, pride has never left our heart because it
is domiciled there, and, to disguise itself: assumes a false
appearance.

And, moreover, we ought also to observe what the
same holy pontiff tells us, that we often fall into this the
worst kind of pride: "Into this fourth kind of pride the
human mind falls very frequently;" and there is no doubt
that it is really a grievous sin, for we thereby offend both
God and our neighbor. And how many men and women
there are, both religious and secular, of every state and

condition, who commit this sin of pride so frequently that it becomes a predominant habit with them.

Practically we notice that all men desire to be distinguished in their own particular art, however inferior it may be, and all seek first to be esteemed as much as others, and then to be distinguished more than others—"I will ascend," each one in his own sphere and also outside his own sphere. The rich man regards himself as greater than the learned man on account of his riches; the learned man as greater than the rich man on account of his learning; the chaste man esteems himself better than the one who gives alms, and the one who gives alms esteems himself more highly than the man who is chaste. Oh, what pride!—and yet few people are willing to recognize that they are proud.

MEDITATION 93

Pride seeks after honors and is grieved when it is despised;
humility is averse to being treated well and rejoices in
contempt, which it knows that it deserves, and its own
uprightness renders it desirous that justice should be done.
Pride never has what it wants, for whatever it possesses,
or has given to it, it considers that it deserves still more;
while humility always thinks it has more than enough, for
it believes that it is unworthy to walk the earth, and that
hell itself is not sufficient punishment for its sins.

—Blessed John of Ávila

☙ † ❧

Pride tempts the great, by giving them to understand that they have attained to their position by their own merit, and that none of their inferiors could be compared with them; it tempts their subordinates, by diverting their attention from their own faults and making them observe and judge the doings of their superiors; they speak nevertheless of and to their superiors with a certain liberty, and as this pride is called a rightful independence in them, so in the superior it is called zeal and decorum.

Sometimes our pride constrains us to talk loud, at other times to preserve a bitter silence. Pride is dissolute in its joys, somber and raving in its melancholy; it seems honorable in appearance, yet is without honor; it is full of valor in giving offense, but cowardly in taking it; it is slow to obey, importunate in its demands to ascertain its duty, but negligent in performing it; while it is prompt to meddle and interfere in all that does not concern it, there is no possibility of bending it in any direction unless it is inclined thereto by its own taste; and it is astute, and pretends to be indifferent about having any office or dignity which it covets, so that it may be forced into accepting them, loving to have those things which it most desires thrust violently upon it for fear it should be regarded with contempt if its desire for them were made known.

MEDITATION 94

Never trust to yourself, either on the ground of experience,
or length of time, or age, or sickness; but always fly
from every occasion of danger as long as you
have strength to raise your eyelids.

–St. Philip Neri

❧ † ☙

After considering pride in itself, it remains for us to observe its effects, and especially seven of the more common and familiar vices which it produces, which are presumption, ambition, envy, vainglory, boastfulness, hypocrisy, and disobedience. Let us examine them with St. Thomas.

Presumption is a vice by which we esteem ourselves able to achieve things beyond our strength, forgetful of the necessity of Divine help. The sinner is guilty of presumption when he believes that he can be converted to God whenever he likes and chooses, as if conversion were the work of his own free-will alone, and living ill yet trusts to make a good death; when he sins and goes on sinning, relying upon obtaining ultimate forgiveness; when he believes that he can of himself, and without the help of grace, both withstand temptation, avoid sin and observe the commandments of God, or else that he can make some supernatural act of faith, hope, charity or contrition, or perform some meritorious act towards his eternal welfare and save himself by persevering in well-doing.

MEDITATION 95

It was right that He should be tempted, that He should suffer with me, to the end that I might know how to conquer when tempted, how to escape when hard pressed. He overcame by force of continence, of faith; He trampled upon ambition, fled from intemperance, bade wantonness be far from Him.

—St. Ambrose

Ambition is a vice which makes us seek our own honor with inordinate avidity. Now, as this honor is a mark of respect and esteem, given to meritorious virtue, and to him who is of superior degree, and as it is certain that we have no merit of ourselves, because everything we receive comes from God, it is not to ourselves, but to God alone that such honor is wholly due.

Moreover, as this honor has been ordained by God as a means to render us capable of helping our neighbor, it is certain that all such honor must be used by us in fulfillment of this end. Two things are needful to enable us to flee from ambition. The first is that we should not appropriate merit of the honor, and the second is that we should confess that this same honor is due wholly to God, and is only dear to us in so far as it can serve our neighbor.

If therefore we are wanting in one of these two things, we commit the sin of ambition. He is ambitious therefore who seeks to have some office or position, whether in the world or in the Church, when he has not the requisite virtue and knowledge to maintain it, and who schemes and plots to be put before others who are more worthy than he.

He is ambitious who desires to be esteemed, honored and revered more than his position merits, and as if he were of higher rank than he is, to be honored as an eloquent preacher or as a clever writer, or in any profession to which he may belong, although in reality he can only be classed amongst the indifferent and mediocre.

MEDITATION 96

*It is necessary to remark that we must conquer some
temptations by contrary acts; for example, temptations to
revenge must be overcome by seeking to do good to those
who have offended you; temptations to vanity by humbling
ourselves; to envy by rejoicing at the good of others.*

–St. Alphonsus Liguori

ᴥ †ᴥ

Envy is a sadness arising from the contemplation of our
neighbor's welfare, when we imagine that the good
which happens to him must be to our own detriment,
prejudicial to our own glory and interest; but of his goods
we only envy those which bring us esteem in the eyes of
the world—riches, dignity, the friendship and favors of the
great, science, praise, fame, and all that which seems to us
to contribute to our credit and to bring us honor.

And it is thus that envy is born within us, when we
see one who is richer, more learned than we are, another
wiser and more virtuous than we, another who has more
talent and ability, and whom therefore we should like to
see deprived of these gifts in order that he might also be
deprived of the praise and honor and any other advan-
tages which we imagine are more due to us than to him.
Now the sin consists in this: that when we ought, from a

sense of charity, to rejoice at our neighbor's prosperity, we are only saddened at it, wishing in our pride that it might be ours, in order that we might be superior to our neighbor in merit; and this sin is the especial sin of the devil, as the Wise Man says, "the envy of the devil," *(Wisdom 2:24)* and therefore the Holy Spirit most justly commands us through St. Paul to guard against it: "Let us not be envying one another," *(Galatians 5:26)* as it is easy to sin mortally in one way or another. But nevertheless, how common this vice is in families, in communities, in every state of life, to high and low, rich and poor, to seculars and even to the Religious themselves!

MEDITATION 97

*We call that vainglory which men take to themselves,
either for what is not in them, or which being in them
is not their own, or which being in them and their
own yet is not worthy of their self-satisfaction.*

–*St. Francis de Sales*

❧ † ☙

Vainglory consists in an inordinate appetite for praise,
and a desire that our merit should shine forth with
glory, and in three different ways this glory can be called
vain and wicked.

Firstly, when we seek to be praised for a virtue or any
other gift of body or soul which we do not possess, or else
to be praised for some frail transitory possession which
is not worthy of praise, such as health, beauty and other
gifts of the body, riches, pomp and other goods which are
called the gifts of fortune.

Secondly, when in seeking praise we value the esteem
and approbation of one whose judgment is unreliable.

Thirdly, when we do not use this praise either for
the honor of God or the good of our neighbor, and this
is always to sin against the dictates of holy Scripture: "Let
us not be made desirous of vainglory," *(Philemon 2:3)* and
it can be a mortal sin when we seek to be praised for
some wrong which we have done or have the intention

of doing, or for some other wrong which we have never done and have had no thought of doing, or else to accept praise for a good which we have not done and which we want to make others believe that we have done; it can also be a mortal sin if we do good only out of human respect with the intention of being seen and praised.

He who suffers from vainglory is in danger of losing his faith also, according to the saying of Christ: "How can you believe who receive glory one from another?" *(John 5:44)*. St. Augustine reflecting upon this, and how little this great evil is known, affirms that none is wiser than he who knows that this love of praise is a vice: "He sees best who sees that love of praise is a vice."

MEDITATION 98

*It is undefined because it never keeps back anything
of its own for itself. When a man boasts of nothing
as his very own, surely all that he has is God's.*

—*St. Bernard of Clarivaux*

❧ † ❧

Boastfulness is a vice by which man, desiring to be
supremely honored above all others, begins to praise
and exalt himself, exaggerating and amplifying things so
as to make his own merit appear greater than it is. It is
also called ostentation, self-praise or forwardness; and
St. Augustine calls it "The worst of all pests;" while St.
Ambrose calls it a net spread by the devil to catch the
strongest and most spiritual: "The devil lays snares such as
entrap the strongest;" and this is a vice which is beyond
measure, because in vaunting ourselves for that which we
have not, we lie to our own conscience and to God; and as
God said of Moab by the prophet: "He is exceeding proud;
I know his boasting, and that the strength thereof is not
according to it" *(Jeremiah 48:29-30).*

It can be a mortal sin when we boast of some sin
which we have committed; when we praise ourselves,
despising others; or else when we praise and exalt ourselves
through an excess of pride which abounds in the heart.

MEDITATION 99

Brethren this pestilence must be avoided that turns
remedies into diseases, medicines into maladies,
holiness into vice, saintliness into sinfulness.

—*St. Peter Chrysologus*

☙ † ❧

Hypocrisy is a vice by which we affect to demon-
strate externally a virtue and a sanctity which we do
not possess; and he is really a hypocrite who, being full of
wickedness within, pretends in his outward appearance to
be good.

There is no vice against which Jesus Christ has
inveighed so much in His Gospel as against this one *(Matthew 6:7, 15, 21)*, condemning it with eight cries of "Woe
unto you," which are eight maledictions. And St. Gregory
remarks that the hypocrites, blinded by pride and hard-
ened in their sins, generally die impenitent without ever
being enlightened, because while we can see that the remedies to the amendment of other vices do good, the disease of hypocrisy is so pestilential that it affects the very
remedies themselves, so that they only serve to foment and
increase the evil.

Hypocrisy is always a mortal sin when we pretend to
be spiritual and holy, and try to appear as such, when we
are not so at heart, caring more for the opinion of men

than for the opinion of God; and it is worse still when we affect sanctity in order to further our own advancement and to acquire credit in order to reach and to work evil; or else to obtain some honor, or other temporal good.

MEDITATION 100

For the obedience shown to the Eternal Father by His Son was greater than the disobedience of a servant to his master, and the humility with which the Son of God died on the Cross redounded more to the honor of the Father than the pride of a servant tended to His injury.

−St. Robert Bellarmine

☙ † ❧

Disobedience is a sin by which we violate the command of our superiors, treating them with contempt, and it can be a mortal sin even in small matters; because, as St. Bernard says, we must not consider the nature of the thing commanded nor the simple transgression of the precept, but the pride of the will which will not submit when it ought. "It is not the simple transgression of the wish but the proud contention of the will that creates criminal disobedience," and the grievousness of the sin can be judged under three different heads.

First, the rank of the superior, because the higher the one who commands, the more grave is the disobedience. It is a greater sin to disobey God than to disobey man, a greater sin to disobey the pope than a bishop, or a father and mother than other relations; and it is also a greater sin to disobey with contempt of the person who commands, than with contempt only of the commandment.

Secondly, in respect of the nature of the things commanded, because when these are of greater importance,
especially in the laws of God, the disobedience is greater,
therefore it is a graver sin to disobey those precepts which
enjoin the love of God than those which command us to
love our neighbor.

PRAYERS FOR HUMILITY

PRAYERS FOR HUMILITY

O Jesus! meek and humble of heart, **Hear me.**
From the desire of being esteemed,
Deliver me, Jesus.

From the desire of being loved...
From the desire of being extolled...
From the desire of being honored...
From the desire of being praised...
From the desire of being preferred to others...
From the desire of being consulted...
From the desire of being approved...
From the fear of being humiliated...
From the fear of being despised...
From the fear of suffering rebukes ...
From the fear of being calumniated ...
From the fear of being forgotten...
From the fear of being ridiculed...
From the fear of being wronged...
From the fear of being suspected...

That others may be loved more than I,
Jesus, grant me the grace to desire it.

That others may be esteemed more than I...
That, in the opinion of the world,
others may increase and I may decrease...
That others may be chosen and I set aside...
That others may be praised and I unnoticed...
That others may be preferred to me in everything...
That others may become holier than I, provided that
I may become as holy as I should...

—Servant of God Cardinal Merry del Val

209

LITANY OF ST. FRANCIS

Lord, have mercy.
    R. Christ, have mercy.
Lord, have mercy.
Christ, hear us.
    R. Christ, graciously hear us.
God, the Father of heaven,
    R. have mercy on us.
God, the Son, the Redeemer of the world,
    R. have mercy on us.
God, the Holy Spirit,
    R. have mercy on us.
Holy Trinity, one God,
    R. have mercy on us.
Holy Mary, conceived without sin,
    R. pray for us.
Sancta Maria, advocate of the Friars minor,
    R. pray for us.
Seraphic Saint Francis,
    R. pray for us.
Saint Francis, Father most prudent,
    R. pray for us.
Saint Francis, patriarch of the poor,
    R. pray for us.
Saint Francis, despising worldly goods,
    R. pray for us.

Saint Francis, model of penance,
> R. pray for us.

Saint Francis, conqueror the vice of the world,
> R. pray for us.

Saint Francis, imitator of our Savior,
> R. pray for us.

Saint Francis, bearer the stigma of Christ,
> R. pray for us.

Saint Francis, marked by the stamp of Jesus,
> R. pray for us.

Saint Francis, standard of purity,
> R. pray for us.

Saint Francis, model of humility,
> R. pray for us.

Saint Francis, way of those going astray,
> R. pray for us.

Saint Francis, remedy of the sick,
> R. pray for us.

Saint Francis, pillar of the Church,
> R. pray for us.

Saint Francis, defender of the faith,
> R. pray for us.

Saint Francis, athlete of Christ,
> R. pray for us.

Saint Francis, bulwark of soldiers,
> R. pray for us.

Saint Francis, invincible shield,
   R. pray for us.

Saint Francis, hammer of heretics,
   R. pray for us.

Saint Francis, conversion of pagans,
   R. pray for us.

Saint Francis, rising up the lame,
   R. pray for us.

Saint Francis, awakening the dead,
   R. pray for us.

Saint Francis, cleansing the lepers,
   R. pray for us.

Saint Francis, rooting out vice,
   R. pray for us.

Saint Francis, agent of divine grace,
   R. pray for us.

Lamb of God, who takest away the sins of the world.
   R. Spare us, O Lord.

Lamb of God, who takest away the sins of the world.
   R. Graciously hear us, O Lord.

Lamb of God, who takest away the sins of the world.
   R. Have mercy on us.

Christ, hear us.
   R. Christ, graciously hear us.

Lord, have mercy.
   R. Christ, have mercy.

Lord, have mercy.
Our Father etc.

V. Pray for us, blessed Francis, our Father,
R. that we may be worthy of the promises of Christ.

V. Lord, hear my prayer,
R. and let my cry come to Thee.

Let us pray:

Extinguish in us the desire for the things of this world, almighty God, and graciously grant that by the intercession of blessed Francis, Father of the poor, being contented with our lot in this life, we may ardently desire those things that are eternal.

Almighty ever-living God, infuse in our hearts the zeal of a chaste humility and a humble chastity, that in imitating our father, blessed Francis, we may serve Thee with a clean heart and body.

O God, whose Church springs forth through the blood of the faithful, graciously pour forth the spirit of our Father saint Francis to us Thy supplicants, that either we may desire to pour forth our blood for Thy Name, or through the virtue of obedience, we may offer to Thee an acceptable sacrifice of ourselves.

O Lord Jesus Christ, when the world was growing cold, in order to inflame our hearts with the fire of Thy love, Thou didst renew the sacred marks of Thy passion on the flesh of our most blessed father Francis; mercifully grant that by his merits and prayers we may always bear our cross, and bring forth worthy fruits of penance. Thou who liveth and reigneth forever and ever. Amen.

PRAYER OF ST. THÉRÈSE FOR HUMILITY

O Jesus! When you were on earth you said: "Learn of Me, for I am meek and humble of heart, and you shall find rest to your souls" *(Matthew 11. 29)*.

O Almighty King of Heaven! My soul indeed finds rest in seeing Thee condescend to wash the feet of Thy Apostles, "having taken the form of a slave" *(Philippians 2. 7)*. I recall the words You uttered to teach me the practise of humility: "I have given you an example, that as I have done to you, so you do also. The servant is not greater than his Lord... If you know these things, you shall be blessed if you do them" *(John 13. 15, 17)*.

I understand, dear Lord, these words which come from Thy meek and humble Heart, and I wish to put them into practice with the help of Thy grace.

I desire to humble myself in all sincerity. I implore Thee, dear Jesus, to send me a humiliation whensoever I try to set myself above others.

And yet, dear Lord, you know my weakness. Each morning I resolve to be humble, and in the evening I recognize that I have often been guilty of pride. The sight of these faults tempts me to discouragement. Yet I know that discouragement itself is a form of pride. I wish, therefore, O my God, to build all my trust upon Thee. As Thou canst do all things, deign to implant in my soul this virtue which I desire. And to obtain it from Thy Infinite Mercy, I will often say to Thee: "Jesus, meek and humble of Heart, make my heart like unto Thine."

THE JESUS PRAYER

Jesus son of God, have mercy on me, a sinner.

PRAYER OF POPE LEO XIII FOR HUMILITY

O Lord, my God, You are all my good, and who am I that I should dare speak to You? I am Your poorest servant and a wretched little worm, much poorer and more contemptible than I can conceive or dare express. Yet remember, O Lord, that I am nothing, I have nothing, and can do nothing. You alone are good, just, and holy: You can do all things, You give all things, You fill all things, leaving only the sinner empty. Remember Your tender mercies, and fill my heart with Your grace. You will not have your works to be empty. How can I support myself in this wretched life, unless Your mercy and grace strengthen me? Turn not Your face from me, delay not Your visitation, withdraw not Your comfort, lest my soul were to become to You as earth without water. O Lord, teach me to do Your will, teach me to converse worthily and humbly in Your sight: for You are my wisdom, Who knows me in truth, and did know me before the world was made, and before I was born into the world.

—Pope Leo XIII

PRAYERS OF ST. THOMAS AQUINAS

Grant me, O Lord my God,
a mind to know you,
a heart to seek you,
wisdom to find you,
conduct pleasing to you,
faithful perseverance in waiting for you,
and a hope of finally embracing you.
Amen.

Lo! upon the Altar lies,
Hidden deep from human eyes,
Angels' Bread from Paradise.

—Lauda Sion

PRAYER OF ST. FRANCIS OF ASSISI
BEFORE A CRUCIFIX

O most High and Glorious God, enlighten the darkness
of my heart. Give me, Lord, a firm faith, sure hope, perfect
love, profound humility—the sing and knowledge so that
I may carry out all of your commandments.

My God and my All! Who art thou, my sweetest Lord
and God? and who am I, a poor little worm, Thy servant?
Most Holy Lord, I wish to love Thee! most sweet Lord,
I wish to love Thee! O Lord my God, I have given Thee
al my heart, and all my body, and I most earnestly desire,
if I only knew how, to do still more for Thy love. Amen.

PRAYER OF ST. ANSELM TO KNOW GOD

O Lord my God,
Teach my heart this day where and how to see you,
Where and how to find you.
You have made me and remade me,
And you have bestowed on me
All the good things I possess,
And still I do not know you.
I have not yet done that
For which I was made.
Teach me to seek you,
For I cannot seek you
Unless you teach me,
Or find you
Unless you show yourself to me.
Let me seek you in my desire,
Let me desire you in my seeking.
Let me find you by loving you,
Let me love you when I find you.
Amen.

MEDIATION OF ST. JOHN FISHER

Rescue me from these manifold perils that I am in, for unless thou wilt of thine infinite goodness relieve me, I am but a lost creature.

PRAYERS OF ST. AUGUSTINE OF HIPPO

Here in this life, O Lord, burn within me, and cut whatsoever You please; here spare me not, provided You do spare and pardon me in eternity.

I know, O Lord, and do with all Humility acknowledge my self an object altogether unworthy of Thy Love; but sure I am, Thou art an Object altogether worthy of mine. I am not good enough to serve Thee, but thou hast a right to the best service I can pay. Do Thou then impart to me some of that Excellence, and that shall supply my own want of worth. Help me to cease from sin according to Thy will, that I may be capable of doing Thee service according to my duty. Enable me so to guard and govern my self, so to begin and finish my course, that when the race of life is run, I may sleep in peace, and rest in Thee. Be with me unto the end, that my sleep may be rest indeed, my rest perfect security, and that security a blessed eternity. Amen.

Lord Jesus, may I know myself and know Thee. I desire nothing other than Thee. May I hate myself and love Thee. May I do all things for Thy sake. May I humble myself and exalt Thee. May I think of nothing but Thee!

Behold how high Thou art, O Lord, and yet dost dwell with the lowly of heart!

AN ACT OF HUMILITY
FROM THE URSULINE MANUAL

Who am I, O God of glory and majesty! who am I that thou shouldst deign even to look on my unworthiness? Whence am I honored with this unspeakable favor that my Lord and my God should come in person to visit me? How shall I, a sinner, a worm of the earth, a mere contemptible nothing venture to approach the God of all sanctity? How shall I presume to eat the bread of angels? Ah Lord! I do not deserve this mark of thy predilection, this additional proof of thy tenderness and love. The consideration of thy exalted greatness and my profound misery, penetrates me with awe and confusion. I have not words to express the sentiments of my heart. With the utmost sincerity, I can only declare the extent of my unworthiness, and admire that infinite goodness which induces thee to stoop to the lowest and basest of thy creatures. O compassionate Lord! thou knowest all my wants, and thou art desirous to relieve them: for this purpose thou hast expressly invited me to approach thy altar, and to become a guest at thy sacred table. Behold I come on thy invitation; I present myself before thee with all my necessities and miseries acknowledging that I am but dust and ashes, and infinitely unworthy that thou shouldst enter under my roof. Whence is this to me? *(Luke 11)*. What is man, O Lord, that thou art mindful of him, or the son of man that thou shouldst visit him? *(Psalm 8)*.

HUMBLE OFFERING OF
ST. MARGARET MARY ALAÇOQUE

Eternal Father,
I offer Thee the submission of Jesus to Thy will,
and I ask of Thee,
through His merits,
the fullness of all grace
and the accomplishment of all Thy holy will.
Blessed be God!

PRAYER OF ST. FERDINAND III OF CASTILE

Thou knowest, O my God, that it is neither from ambition nor the love of glory that I make war on the enemies of Thy name, but in order to strike terror into those that blaspheme it.

PRAYER OF ST. EPHREM

O Lord and Master of my life, spare me fro the spirit of apathy and meddling, of idle chatter and love of power. Instead, grant to me, your servant, the spirit of integrity and humility, of patience and love. yes, O Lord and God, grant me the grace to be aware of my sins and not to judge others, for you are blessed, now and ever and forever. Amen.

PRAYERS OF ST. THOMAS MORE

Almighty Jesus, my sweet Savior Christ, who would graciously agree to wash the feet of your twelve apostles with your own almighty hands, not only of the good but also of the traitor himself; graciously agree, good Lord, of your excellent goodness, in such wise to wash the foul feet of my affections that I, with humility and charity for the love of you, never have such pride enter into my heart as to disdain either in friend or foe to defile my hands with washing of their feet.

Give me the grace, Good Lord to set the world at naught. To set the mind firmly on You and not to hang upon the words of men's mouths. To be content to be solitary. Not to long for worldly pleasures. Little by little utterly to cast off the world and rid my mind of all its business.

Not to long to hear of earthly things, but that the hearing of worldly fancies may be displeasing to me. Gladly to be thinking of God, piteously to call for His help. To lean into the comfort of God. Busily to labor to love Him.

To know my own vileness and wretchedness. To humble myself under the mighty hand of God. To bewail my sins and, for the purging of them, patiently to suffer adversity. Gladly to bear my purgatory here. To be joyful in tribulations. To walk the narrow way that leads to life.

To have the last thing in remembrance. To have ever before my eyes my death that is ever at hand. To make death no stranger to me. To foresee and consider the ever-lasting fire of Hell. To pray for pardon before the judge comes. To have continually in mind the passion that Christ suffered for me.

For His benefits unceasingly to give Him thanks.

To buy the time again that I have lost. To abstain from vain conversations. To shun foolish mirth and gladness. To cut off unnecessary recreations. Of worldly substance, friends, liberty, life and all, to set the loss at naught, for the winning of Christ.

To think my worst enemies my best friends, for the brethren of Joseph could never have done him so much good with their love and favor as they did him with their malice and hatred. These minds are more to be desired of every man than all the treasures of all the princes and kings, Christian and heathen, were it gathered and laid together all in one heap. Amen *(Tower Prayer)*

PRAYER OF ST. ALPHONSUS LIGUORI FOR PATIENCE

Give me patience and resignation in difficulties and in contradictions. Give me the spirit of mortifying myself for Thy love. Give me the spirit of true humility, that I may even rejoice in being considered vile and full of faults. Teach me to do Thy will, and then tell me what Thou wil-iest of me, for I will do all.

PRAYER OF ST. LOUIS DE MONTFORT TO OUR LADY FOR HUMILITY

Hail Mary, beloved daughter of the Eternal Father. Hail Mary, admirable mother of the Son. Hail Mary, faithful Spouse of the Holy Ghost. Hail Mary, my mother, my loving mistress, my powerful sovereign. Destroy in me all that may displease God; root it up and bring it to nought. May thy profound humility take the place of my pride. May thy virtues take the place of my sins; may thy merits be my only adornment in the sight of God and make up for all that is wanting in me. I do not ask thee for visions, revelations, sensible devotions, or spiritual pleasures. It is thy privilege to dispose of all the gifts of God, just as thou willest. I wish for nothing other than that which was thine, to believe sincerely without spiritual pleasures, to suffer joyfully without human consolation, to die continually to myself without respite, and to work zealously and unselfishly for thee until death, as the humblest of thy servants. Amen.

PRAYER OF ST. BERNARD OF CLAIRVAUX

I give thanks to Thee, O Lord Jesus, that Thou hast deigned to admit me at least to perceive that odor so sweet. Yea, Lord, so let me be admitted, even as the dogs, though of such small account, are allowed to eat of the crumbs which fall from their master's table.

PRAYER OF ST. TERESA OF ÁVILA FOR PATIENCE

O Lord, how true that all harm comes to us from not keeping our eyes fixed on You; if we were to look at nothing else but the way, we would soon arrive. But we meet with a thousand falls and obstacles and lose the way because we don't keep our eyes—as I say—on the true way. It seems so new to us that you would think we had never walked on it. It's certainly something to excite pity, that which sometimes happens. Teach me, my God, to suffer in peace the afflictions which You send me that my soul may emerge form the crucible like gold, both brighter and purer, to find You within me. Amen.

PRAYER OF ST. CHARLES BORROMEO

Almighty God, you have generously made known to human beings the mysteries of your life through Jesus Christ your Son in the Holy Spirit. Enlighten my mind to know these mysteries which your Church treasures and teaches. Move my heart to love them and my will to live in accord with them. Give me the ability to teach this Faith to others without pride, without ostentation, and without personal gain. Let me realize that I am simply your instrument for bringing others to the knowledge of the wonderful things you have done for all your creatures.

Help me to be faithful to this task that you have entrusted to me. Amen.

THE HUMILITY OF THE BLESSED VIRGIN MARY

The Magnificat

My soul doth magnify the Lord.

And my spirit hath rejoiced in God my Saviour.

Because he hath regarded the humility of his handmaid; for behold from henceforth all generations shall call me blessed.

Because he that is mighty, hath done great things to me; and holy is his name.

And his mercy is from generation unto generations, to them that fear him.

He hath shewed might in his arm: he hath scattered the proud in the conceit of their heart.

He hath put down the mighty from their seat, and hath exalted the humble.

He hath filled the hungry with good things; and the rich he hath sent empty away.

He hath received Israel his servant, being mindful of his mercy:

As he spoke to our fathers, to Abraham and to his seed for ever.

PANGE LINGUA OF FORTUNATUS

All within a lowly manger,
lo, a tender babe He lies!
see his gentle Virgin Mother
lull to sleep his infant cries!
while the limbs of God incarnate
round with swathing bands she ties.

PRAYERS FROM THE ROMAN MISSAL

O Lord, I am not worthy that thou shalt enter under my roof, but only say the word and my soul shall be healed.

O Lord, may we not be proud-minded, but to make progress by pleasing humility; that despising what is evil, we may exercise with free charity the things which are right. Through Christ Our Lord.

Lord Jesus Christ, take all my freedom, my memory, my understanding, and my will. All that I have and cherish Thou hast given me. I surrender it all to be guided by Thy will. Thy grace and Thy love are wealth enough for me. Give me these Lord Jesus and I ask for nothing more. Amen. –St. Ignatius of Loyola

PRAYER TO GOD TO IMITATE
THE HUMILITY OF THE BLESSED VIRGIN

O blessed God! It was her humility that has thus exalted the Virgin Mary in Thy favor and made her thus glorious in heaven! It was this, that first turned Thy eyes upon her, and singled her out to be the subject of thy infinite love and power!

And what then is it, O God, we do! We pretend to the hopes of heaven, and seem to expect thy grace, in order to help us in our way; but where is our humility, which may turn Thy eyes towards us, and move Thee to stretch forth Thy hand of power in order to our help! Where is our humility!

In all circumstances, our vain inclinations and our pride unlooked for, discover themselves. But where is our humility! We can easily show that, which Thy soul hates, O God; that which turns away Thy eyes from us, and shuts up Thy ears against our prayers; where is our lowly and humble heart, that draws Thy regard upon us and prepares our souls to be exalted in Thy favor, and in heaven?

Grant us, O God, to be thus wise and industrious against this evil; and now on this festival of humility glorified, with a bountiful hand pour forth into our souls the spirit of a solid and true humility, even a portion of that which prepared the soul of the Blessed Virgin to become a treasure of so many graces. Amen.

O Holy Virgin, most spotless mirror of humility; by that exceeding charity which moved thee to visit thy holy cousin St. Elizabeth; obtain for us, by thy intercession, that our hearts may be so visited by thy most holy Son, that free from all sin, we may praise him, and give him thanks forever. Amen.

O God, Thou who looks down upon low and knows the lofty from afar, grant to Thy servants that they would always, and with a pure heart, follow the humility of the Blessed Virgin Mary who pleased Thee with her Virginity and with her humility, conceived Thy Son, Our Lord, Jesus Christ. Amen.

PRAYER TO ST. PHILIP NERI FOR HUMILITY

O my glorious patron, Saint Philip, thou who wast so humble as to consider thyself a useless servant and unworthy of human praise but deserving the contempt of all, to such a degree as to renounce by every means the honors offered thee on numerous occasions by the Supreme Pontiffs themselves, thou seest what an exaggerated esteem I have for myself, how readily I judge and think ill of others, how ambitious I am even in well-doing, and how much I allow myself to be disturbed and influenced by the good or bad opinion which others entertain of me. Dear Saint, obtain for me a truly humble heart, so that I may rejoice at being despised, may feel no resentment at being overlooked, nor be unduly elated by praise, but rather let me seek to be great in the eyes of God alone. Amen.

PRAYER OF ST. FRANCIS BORGIA

I summon Thee, then, O my God, to enlighten my spirit, and to inspire me with sentiments of sincere humility, that after the example of holy Job, I may say to the dust: "Thou art my father; and to the worms, Ye are my brothers;" that thus I may be convinced I can do nothing without Thee, that Thou art my only refuge and my sovereign good. Amen.

SCRIPTURE VERSES
FOR HUMILITY

SCRIPTURE VERSES FOR HUMILITY

Learn of Me, because I am meek and humble of heart, and you shall find rest to your souls.
—Matthew 11:29

Everyone that exalteth himself shall be humbled, and he that humbleth himself shall be exalted.
—Luke 14:11

God resisteth the proud, and giveth grace to the humble.
—James 4:6

Where pride is, there also shall be reproach, but where humility is, there also is wisdom.
—Proverbs 11:2

Thus saith the Lord: Cursed be the man that trusteth in man, and maketh flesh his arm, and whose heart departeth from the Lord.
—Jeremias 17:5

Lord, my heart is not exalted, nor are my eyes lofty; neither have I walked in great matters, nor in wonderful things above me.
—Psalm 130:1

The greater thou art, the more humble thyself in all things, and thou shalt find grace before God.
—Ecclesiasticus 3:20

To whom shall I have respect but to him that is poor and little and of contrite heart, and that trembleth at my words.
—*Isaias 46:2*

If thou hast received them, why dost thou glory as though they were thine, and as if thou hadst not received them.
—*1 Corinthians 4:7*

It is good for me, O Lord, that Thou hast humbled me, that I may learn Thy justifications.
—*Psalm 118 [119]: 71*

For Thy sake, O God of Israel, I have borne reproach.
—*Psalm 68 [69]: 9*

Unless the Lord had been my helper, my soul had almost dwelt in hell.
—*Psalm 93 [94]*

I will speak to the Lord, whereas I am but dust and ashes.
—*Genesis 18:27*

And why dost thou exalt thyself, dust and ashes!
—*Sirach 10:9*

Serving the Lord with all humility, and with tears, and temptations which befell me.
—*Acts 20:19*

The pride of them that hate thee ascendeth continually.
—*Psalm 73[74]:23*

The fruit of humility is the fear of the Lord, riches and glory and life.
—*Proverbs 22:4*

Boast not against the branches. But if thou boast, thou bearest not the root, but the root (bearest) thee.
—*Romans 11:18*

Humiliation followeth the proud: and glory shall uphold the humble of spirit.
—*Proverbs 29:23*

Before destruction, the heart of a man is exalted: and before he be glorified, it is humbled.
—*Proverbs 18:12*

The fear of the Lord is the lesson of wisdom: and humility goeth before glory.
—*Proverbs 15:33*

Unless you become as little children, you cannot enter the kingdom of heaven.
—*Matthew 18:3*

It is better to be humbled with the meek, than to divide spoils with the proud.
—*Proverbs 16:19*

Walk not as also the Gentiles walk, in the vanity of their mind.
—*Ephesians 4:17*

To whom shall I have respect but to him that is poor and little, and that trembleth at my words?
—*Isaias 66:2*

Lord, I am not worthy that thou shouldst enter under my roof: but only say the word, and my servant shall be healed.
—*Matthew 8:8*

He must increase, but I must decrease.
—*John 3:30*

Let not the foot of pride come to me.
—*Psalm 35 [36]:12*

Woe to him that gainsayeth his maker, a sherd of the earthen pots: shall the clay say to him that fashioneth it: What art thou making, and thy work is without hands?
—*Isaias 45:9*

The Lord maketh poor and maketh rich, he humbleth and he exalteth.
— *1 Kings [1 Samuel] 2:7*

With all humility and mildness, with patience, supporting one another in charity.
—*Ephesians 4:2*

Not minding high things, but consenting to the humble. Be not wise in your own conceits.
—*Romans 12:16*

Be humbled in the sight of the Lord, and he will exalt you.
—Romans 4:10

Let nothing be done through contention, neither by vain glory: but in humility, let each esteem others better than themselves.
—Philippians 2:3

Let no man seduce you, willing in humility, and religion of angels, walking in the things which he hath not seen, in vain puffed up by the sense of his flesh.
—Acts 2:18

And thou saidst in thy heart: I will ascend into heaven, I will exalt my throne above the stars of God, I will sit in the mountain of the covenant, in the sides of the north. I will ascend above the height of the clouds, I will be like the most High.
—Isaias 14:13-14

The Lord of hosts hath designed it, to pull down the pride of all glory, and bring to disgrace all the glorious ones of the earth.
—Isaias 23:9

And after that he was in distress he prayed to the Lord his God: and did penance exceedingly before the God of his fathers.
—2 Paralipomenon [Chronicles] 33:12

Whose adorning let it not be the outward plaiting of the hair, or the wearing of gold, or the putting on of apparel: But the hidden man of the heart in the incorruptibility of a quiet and a meek spirit, which is rich in the sight of God.
—*1 Peter 3:3-4*

Be you humbled therefore under the mighty hand of God, that he may exalt you in the time of visitation.
—*1 Peter 5:6*

For he that hath been humbled, shall be in glory: and he that shall bow down his eyes, he shall be saved.
—*Job 22:29*

And thy heart was softened, and thou hast humbled thyself in the sight of God for the things that are spoken against this place, and the inhabitants of Jerusalem, and reverencing my face, hast rent thy garments, and wept before me: I also have heard thee, saith the Lord.
—*2 Paralipomenon [Chronicles] 34:27*

He that cometh from above, is above all. He that is of the earth, of the earth he is, and of the earth he speaketh. He that cometh from heaven, is above all.
—*John 3:31*

Therefore, when thou dost an almsdeed, sound not a trumpet before thee, as the hypocrites do in the synagogues and in the streets, that they may be honoured by men.
—*Matthew 6:2*

For the Son of man also is not come to be ministered unto, but to minister, and to give his life a redemption for many.
—*Mark 10:45*

But the foolish things of the world hath God chosen, that he may confound the wise; and the weak things of the world hath God chosen, that he may confound the strong. And the base things of the world, and the things that are contemptible, hath God chosen, and things that are not, that he might bring to nought things that are: That no flesh should glory in his sight.
—*1 Corinthians 27-29*

He hath put down the mighty from their seat, and hath exalted the humble.
—*Luke 1:52*

For the Lord is high, and looketh on the low: and the high he knoweth afar off.
—*Psalm 137 [138]:6*

And said to them: Whosoever shall receive this child in my name, receiveth me; and whosoever shall receive me, receiveth him that sent me. For he that is the lesser among you all, he is the greater.
—*Luke 9:48*

Be subject to the ancients. And do you all insinuate humility one to another.
—*1 Peter 5:5*

If any man desire to be first, he shall be the last of all, and be minister of all.
—*Mark 9:34*

For it is written: As I live, saith the Lord, every knee shall bow to me, and every tongue shall confess to God.
—*Romans 14:11*

If then I being your Lord and Master, have washed your feet; you also ought to wash one another's feet.
—*Romans 13:14*

BIBLIOGRAPHY

BIBLIOGRAPHY

Assisi, Francis of, Saint, *Works of the Seraphic Father St. Francis of Assisi*, London, R. Washbourne, 1882

Aquinas, Thomas, Saint, Catena *Aurea*, Siena, Cantagalli, 1954

Ávila, John of, *Letters of Blessed John of Ávila*, London, Burns and Oats Ltd., 1904

Ávila, Teresa of, Saint, *The Interior Castle*, Charlotte, NC, TAN Books, 2011

Bagnoregio, Bonaventure, of, Saint, *Holiness of Life*, St. Louis, Herder Book Co., 1928

Bellarmine, Robert F., Saint, *The Seven Words Spoken on the Cross*—De arte bene moriendi, Paris, Sebastian Cramoisy, 1620

Bergamo, Gaetano Maria, Fra, *Humility of Heart*, Charlotte, TAN Books, 1978

Borgia, Francis, Saint, *The Spiritual Works of St. Francis Borgia*, London, Thomas Richardson and Sons, 1875

Catholic Church, *The Holy Bible*, translated from the Latin Vulgate; Rockford, TAN Books and Publishers, 1971

Clairvaux, Bernard, of, Saint, *St. Bernard's sermons on the Canticle of Canticles*, Dublin, Browne and Nolan, 1920
  –On Loving God, South Wales, Tenby, 1911

Cross, John, of the, Saint, *The Dark Night of the Soul*, Charlotte, TAN Books, 2010

Fisher, John, Saint, *Commentary on the Seven Penitential Psalms*, London, Manresa Press, 1915

Johnson, Francis, *Voices of the Saints Counsels from the Saints to bring comfort and guidance in daily living*, Charlotte, NC, TAN Books, 1986

The Lady's Primer, or office of the Blessed Virgin Mary, Ormskirk, 1891

Leo XIII, Pope, *The Practice of Humility*, London, Burns and Oates Ltd., 1898

Liguori, Alphonsus, Saint, *Preparation for death, or considerations on the eternal maxims: useful for all as meditations and serviceable to priests for sermons*, London, Burns and Oates, 1867
  –*Sermons of St. Alphonsus Liguori for all the Sundays of the year*, Charlotte, NC, TAN Books, 1982
  –*The True Spouse of Jesus Christ*, Brooklyn, Redemptorist Fathers, 1929
  –*Uniformity with God's Will*, Charlotte, TAN Books, 2013

de Lisieux, Thérèse, Saint, *The Story of a Soul: the autobiography of St. Thérèse of Lisieux*, Charlotte, NC, TAN Books, 2012

   —Saint *Thoughts of Saint Thérèse: the Little Flower of Jesus, Carmelite of the Monastery of Lisieux*, 1873-1897, Charlotte, NC, TAN Books, 1988

De Montfort, Louis-Marie Grignion, Saint, *True Devotion to Mary: With preparation for Total Consecration*, Charlotte, TAN Books, 2010

Prayers for Sundays, Holidays and other festivals, from Low Sunday to the 21st Sunday after Pentecost, Dublin, John Gother, 1704

Pius V, *Missale Romanum*, Rome, 1903

De Sales, Francis, *Introduction to the Devout Life*, Charlotte, TAN Books, 2012

   —*Treatise on the Love of God*, Charlotte, TAN Books, 2012

The Ursuline Manual, or a Collection of Prayers, Spiritual Exercises and Various Instructions, Dublin, Ric Coyne, 1841